POETRY IN THE PARKS

A Celebration of the National Parks of
England and Wales in Poems and Photographs

Edited by Wendy Bardsley

Published by Sigma Leisure – an imprint of
Sigma Press, 1 South Oak Lane, Wilmslow, Cheshire SK9 6AR, England.

British Library Cataloguing in Publication Data
A CIP record for this book is available from the British Library.

ISBN: 1-85058-711-6

Typesetting and Design by: Sigma Press, Wilmslow, Cheshire.

Cover Design: The Agency, Macclesfield

Cover Photograph: Evening, Llangorse Lake, The Brecon Beacons *(David Brinn)*

Back cover photograph of Wendy Bardsley: Mike Frisbee

Printed by: MFP Design & Print

Foreword

– by Alan Howarth CBE MP, Minister for the Arts

It seems entirely appropriate that the 50th birthday of the National Parks should be celebrated in verse. Both stunning landscape and telling verse have the power to lift us out of the everyday and allow us to escape the humdrum: both are inspiring. The concise richness of poetry conveys the essence and spirit of a place admirably, and so it is that the amazing variety of landscape portrayed here has inspired a literary diversity that is equally impressive – from Samuel Coleridge to Sylvia Plath, and from Ted Hughes to Mike Harding.

Some of these poems were composed long before the establishment of the National Parks in 1951 but describe a landscape that had evolved only slowly up to that time. Had the then Labour government not acted to preserve these outstanding aspects of our natural heritage, the poetry may well have proved more enduring than the countryside which inspired it. I trust that I may be allowed to applaud the foresight of my predecessors.

Enduring, diverse and inspiring – our National Parks and the poetry included here are all of these, but they also share the power to enrich our lives. I hope that your pleasure in these evocative words and photographs will prompt you to visit the National Parks and experience their magnificence at first-hand. Perhaps you will then discover, as Wordsworth did, that long after your visit such beauty has the power to 'flash upon that inward eye' and to fill your heart with pleasure. I do hope so, for it is that appreciation and joy that will help preserve our National Parks long into the new millennium.

Alan Howarth

For John Ward, 1915-1999

Preface

Compiling this book has given me great pleasure. Poetry, I believe, is where feelings, thoughts and words come together in the best and most triumphant way. Through our National Parks and the poetry here we can celebrate our uniquely beautiful world.

Not only do our Parks give immense joy to those who visit them, they are also a source of much creative output in ways other than writing, with many people working together on different tasks, from ranging and caring for wildlife, woodland and water, to keeping the libraries and information services interesting and up to date. I have been both moved and spurred on by the sensitive and inspiring introductions sent to me for each of the sections. They are almost poems in themselves.

The search for poetry has sometimes been exhausting, since getting the right selection has been very important. I have tried to offer different ways of looking. Some of the poems are personal or domestic, comical and imaginative, spiritual and universal, and on occasion perhaps even cosmic!

We are all familiar with Wordsworth's 'Daffodils'. Yet Wordsworth by no means had his head in the clouds. He was in fact actively concerned about the lives of the people around him, as well as the countryside, and is thought to have had the initial idea of creating national parks in Britain, one of the first being The Lake District where he lived from 1813 to 1850. At the present time, ten of our Parks have official status, The Broads, a special wetland, being a park in all but name.

The United States was the first country to take care of its wild and unspoilt places, setting up the Yellowstone Park in 1872, with others to follow. A lot of the poets anthologised here are well known. What is sometimes not so known is the passion they have for the land. Our love of the planet is a way the earth can unite us. Read and enjoy!

Wendy Bardsley.

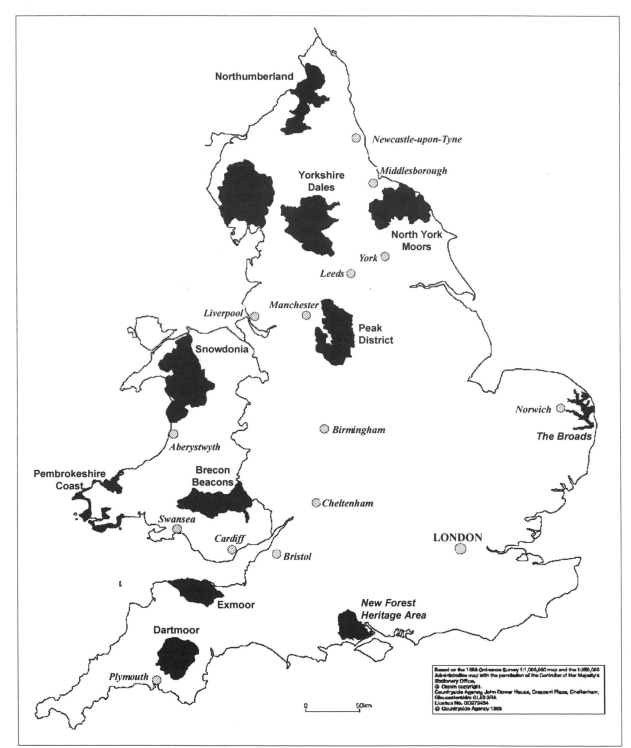

National Parks, The Broads and the New Forest Heritage Area *(by kind permission of The Countryside Agency)*

Contents

Introduction

Ewen Cameron, Chairman, The Countryside Agency

Britain has some of the finest countryside in the world and our rural heritage is deeply engrained in our nationhood. Important parts of our literature, art and music are bedded in our love of nature, open air, the rural vernacular, the history of our surroundings and the changing nature of our countryside.

The most beautiful, spectacular and dramatic expanses of the country have been given National Park status in recognition of their importance and special value in our crowded island. Combining the natural topography with the rich patterns of landscape created by farmers and landowners over many generations, they are an important part of our cultural heritage that has been protected for all to enjoy.

But protecting these finest areas is not an easy task, for the countryside is a living and evolving entity. The establishment of the first National Parks during the 1950s was the culmination of a campaign that is part of our political history. Today, new National Parks are being proposed in Scotland and the south-east of England, reflecting concerns in society that we must hand on to future generations what the nation has inherited with all its richness intact.

The poems and photographs in 'Poetry in the Parks' provide the reader with inspiration as well as appreciation of the variety of the landscape and its moods. Those who have captured the beauty in poignant words and stunning images conserve its splendour at a given moment, reminding us of the long interaction between man and the environment.

As one progresses through the Parks in these pages it is impossible not to be impressed by the diversity of beauty. Society must ensure that all British people, and our guests from overseas, can enjoy the quality of our countryside without damaging the very fabric that makes it so special. Awareness and understanding will ensure that the National Parks, and the creative output they inspire, are safe for the future. It is against this background that the Countryside Agency works with local communities and others to protect our finest landscapes.

Ewen Cameron

The Brecon Beacons

The Brecon Beacons National Park, like all other National Parks in England and Wales, is a "working" landscape, where people have lived and worked for thousands of years. What we see today as a harmonious blend of natural beauty and human history has evolved over centuries as a result of the interaction between man and the land. The Park's beauty is a blend of dramatic scenery, wildlife and a fascinating past.

It is a landscape of contrasts with wild, open moorland and hidden waterfalls, windswept mountains and sheltered valleys, bustling market towns and isolated farmsteads. Farming dominates the landscape and Welsh cultural traditions are strong. This agricultural landscape is rich in wildlife habitats with a wonderful variety of plants and animals, both common and internationally rare.

There is a powerful sense of history in the legacy of ancient monuments and buildings telling the story of the people who have lived and worked here during the last five thousand years.

The designation of the Brecon Beacons as a National Park in 1957 recognised the outstanding qualities of the landscape. On behalf of us all, the National Park Authority works to ensure that the Park remains a special place – for the people who live and work here and for visitors, both now and in the future.

Bernard Watkins, Assistant National Park Officer (Visitor Services)

Jazz Festival

What I am trying to say
Looks foolish, doesn't it,
With all this noise going on?
The town has been charmed with jazz,
Like a chameleon, putting its mouth
Just so. Have you understood
What it says?
        Each of us has ears and
Some persuasiveness. Do you think
We need such a rumpus
In the small hours of the afternoon?
Or are we slowly remembering something
Of the vainglorious shapes of riot
Which the shuffling out-island slaves
Would put on when Picton had
The reins in Trinidad.
      I cross the bridge
Leaving the town. The Usk
Is thin and willowy. The martins
Make their holes in the bank
Just as usual. Why should I listen
More fervently when the town fixes its
Walls around me, though I hear nothing
But the vexed bass?
      When I was jaunty
And unafraid, the river hill was
Dinas, staining the right bank
With shadow, canvassing the sticks
About the edge. But what is the dismal
Sum of this itinerary? Is there some
Happy issue, of the town as well
As the river? Or should it be this humbling
Bass? Could it be assumed
That time and his friends do not
Make mistakes?

Roland Mathias

My Son on Castell Dinas

Later, we walked up to the dinas holding hands.
Fosse, tump and cliff, erupted meeting place
of limestone and red sand,
grass sheepshitten, sheepcropped,
hawthorn and decaying fences.
Eastward, the track along the ridge
and all its folds of mountain falling north.
Westward, mynydd troed across the bwlch
hard and darkening in late afternoon.

The cessna towed a glider overhead
snorting in laborious air.
Its shadow rippled on the pant
and the gravel droning died.

Released, he ran and played and made discoveries
and cairns and cromlechs
from the shale of fallen towers.

I saw grass and earth and stone
lichened, split, layered like the name.
Castell — men in helmets holding natives down.
Dinas — city before rome breathed.
Cattle, slaves and iron bars.

A mile of air fell down towards the farms
blurring smoky in the shade.
Above the cup of land and ring of scarp,
high, the glider's lazy tilt and wheel
caught late sun on the wings,
glass teardrop of cockpit gleaming
pearly as aluminium.

He rampaged on the parapets,
slipped from my reaching hand
cartooned to thirty yards of shadow.

I watched the ridge of mynydd troed turn black,
the tugplane dropping in to shadow
trailing rope.

Christopher Meredith

a *bwlch* is a gap and *pant* a hollow

Quarry

The long lines of their edges
interlace in the haze, bare
masses of sandstone, clouds
of rock.
        The scoop of glaciers
is nothing here. Yesterday
they melted. It is desert one feels
under the short brown grass. The surprise,
to find, broken off in mid air,
solid rivers – the silted lenses,
the sense of invisible sources.

In this quarry, a group of us stand
below the earliest of plants,
black strands of life,
spore-heads in the stone.
On this ground, our forebears
never set foot. The worst,
and more than the worst, might already
have happened: nothing but elements,
heatings and freezings, continents
adrift, breaking.
        But in rock
at our feet, fine-grained as flesh,
is the swirl of a single wave.

How the sun flows over it, a flutter
of gold in the summer air.
It would have been beautiful, that fine
film of clear water.

Not hard to believe. But eyes
were not made then. Millennia
were still to align the molecules
in striations of ice.
        We are early
humans, between glaciations, trying
to see. Cities are suddenly
myths we barely remember.
More real, these fibres, enlarged
for our staining eyes and angled
to catch how daylight fell,
once, on their ribs and knotches.

We are grateful to see this, life
leaving its mark in the silent
upheavals. But the layer that will hold
us may be thinner, with black
deposits sealing it, and graves

5

of our kind inexplicably massed.

Instructed to test the rock
for silt or mud, we crumble
pieces in our teeth. It is mudstone,
smooth, without taste. The river
flows again, thickening, messageless
on our tongues.
                    There is time
for it all to happen again.

Or not.

                    A drift of seed
hesitates in the quarry mouth
meeting the still cold.
Light catches it.
                    As I watch,
my brain is an estuary, shallow,
dazzled with plankton, cells
at the tide's mercy, idling.

Matter watching itself.

Anne Cluysenaar

Goddess of Craig Cwm-Ilwch

On a day as sun-charmed as this
You might want to trust her. Fatal mistake.
She who appears so beneficent has a past.

Although I might lie down on her baking hillside,
Sport among newts in her sparkle-water tarn,
Push from my mind

That she is a moody goddess
Who, suddenly spleenful, may pull down evil weather,
Drench her domain in danger

Even for dauntless SAS commandos,
Upstarts she hoods in mist
Sometimes to death,

I can never forget how she concealed for a month
The body of five-year-old Tommy Jones,
His obelisk pinned in contrition now at her throat.

Frances Nagle

The Brecon Beacons: The Usk Valley *(David Brinn, Brecon Beacons National Park)*

The Brecon Beacons *(David Brinn, Brecon Beacons National Park)*

The Brecon Beacons: Llyn y Fan Fach *(David Brinn, Brecon Beacons National Park)*

The Morning-Watch

O joys? Infinite sweetness! with what flowers,
And shoots of glory, my soul breaks, and buds!
       All the long hours
       Of night, and rest
       Through the still shrouds
       Of sleep, and clouds.
    This dew fell on my breast;
       O how it *bloods*.
And *spirits* all my earth! hark! In what rings,
And *hymning circulations* the quick world
       Awakes, and sings;
       The rising winds.
       And falling springs,
       Birds, beasts, all things
    Adore him in their kinds.
       Thus all is hurled
In sacred *hymns*, and *order,* the great *chime*
And *symphony* of nature. Prayer is
       The world in tune,
       A spirit-voice,
       And vocal joys
    Whose echo is heaven's bliss.
       O let me climb
When I lie down! The pious soul by night
Is like a clouded star, whose beams though said
       To shed their light
       Under some cloud
       Yet are above,
       And shine, and move
    Beyond that misty shroud.
       So in my bed
That curtained grave, though sleep, like ashes, hide
My lamp, and life, both shall in thee abide.

Henry Vaughan

On Pen y Fan

I will not lift up my eyes to mountains.
To walk on hills is to parade your arrogance.
Is to look down on people.
Yet all peaks are relative;
It depends on your viewpoint.

Aircraft look down and sneer at mountain tops,
Their pilots wink at the altimeter's dark eye.
But aircraft crash before landing,
Or shortly after take off.
Put not your trust in turbines.

At Newport generators jerk current
Down miles of cables, coils, and wire capillaries.
Bold electricians switch and cut.
But circuits short and stutter.
Routine maintenance sets in.

At Merthyr assembly lines are tamer —
New machines make tools to tool yet unmade machines.
Parallel men serve them in rows,
With some sacrifices and
Mechanical obedience.

Even Breconshire hills are mechanised,
Triangulated, probed, trudged over and contoured.
What for? Tourists kill time climbing
Or walking. Soft substitute.
A mountain is a machine.

Brian Morris

Pool of the Witch, Talgarth

Go out beyond the hospital's main gate, turn
to your left. Proceed upstream along the lane.
Find where to leave the car, lodged high above
the tree-tops and busy stream. Put on stout boots;

pass through the smaller gate to take the path
that leads to Pwll y Wrach. Now see how thin
the clustering trees become as they yearn upwards for
the anvil-dapple of the ambered light;

where there are sunbeams, look for veils
where filtered beams and vaporous air
weave swathes on swathes of wavery voiles.

Proceed along the downward track. Watch,
and you'll catch the glint of fallen
feathers as you listen for the birdcall
and the rising chorus: barely

distinguishable, at first the water's fall is
just another murmur
mingled with the sounds of trees
and the coming season's fragrant breeze
winding among the bending grasses;

clamber down past earth and stone,
come close almost enough to touch
and taste the veiled white clamour
> where the two spectra
> as bright chords of water
pitch and call towards the churning cauldron
cooled by translucent waters' spume and fall

where the healing Salamander coils
and endlessly consumes her fiery tail.

Angela Morton

The Wizard's Loss

(After Sgwd Gwladus, or The Lady's Fall, Brecon Beacons)

He had worn her to shadow,
The wind howling
Down the moor of his back,
Her pink cheeks gone,
Her form no more
Than an occasional
Shudder.

In this dream
She was raw darkness,
Some days dressed in black silk,
Her attendants
Singing a mass.

The thick beat
Of his heart
Had done it,
In a fit
Of anger.
A hollow sound in which
He feared there was nothing.

*

In his obnoxious apothecary
He kept Vomica,
Vermilion,
The precipitate of arsenic,
Which he had once served her,
Whisking the whites
From the eggs of plover after,
To restore her strength,
Waiting anxiously for her to recover.

Later he climbed the four winds,
Looking for peace offerings;
Harebells, primroses,
The fresh tresses of sunbeams,
To take back
As gifts.

For he was all desire.
His passion such
As would strip the skin from the limbs of Eros.

And he knew she knew,
Seeing the terrible glare in his eyes,
As she ate the fruits of his labours;
Woodland berries, wild mushrooms,

The hips of roses
Gathered from Neuadd gardens,
The tiny bones of crustaceans
Scattered
In the cave of their kitchen,
His own choice seas.

*

Yet, he did not trust her.
Wherever she went
His jealousy aimed its backward arrow,
His face turning to stone,
Consuming her,
As he consumed himself.

And he despised himself,
His habits inward,
Scarcely daring to raise his eyes
To her beauty,
Her arms braceleted in gold,
The lobes of her ears
Dripping gems
From the deepest caverns,
Her dark hair wound in coral.

There were days
He felt himself beggarly;
Ill-grown from some twisted plot,
Lifeless for months,
Curled up
Like a small furred creature
Deep in sleep.

Till the centre of a fit and start
Entered him; a prodigious power
bringing the clatter of blood.

*

Though he was too long gone ...

*

It is common now for him to find her,
Lying up in sunlight,
In a nook or cranny of rock.
He covets the pale blood in her veins,
Whatever it is
Provides her stillness;
That translucent antiquity.

She has decided herself
A Daphnia,
Cloning her own daughters,
Her own mothers.

Sex is simple.
She enters it self-congratulatory,
Like a song that sticks in the same groove,
Over and over.
Whilst he,
Fearful for his progeny,

Lurches nightly,

Like a great bird,

On the plume of her Fall.

Wendy Bardsley

Brecon

It reminds me of somewhere else.
The expanse of sky is greater than the ground.
Spongy ledges of heather give
an acid catch of peat.

Kate dawdles down the hill
open hands droop
claim to have no knowledge
of ever having had the map.

There are marks of farmers
red slopes swelling into green
wisps of wool on barbed wire
skidding clouds reflected in hidden pleats of water.

I remember climbing over a gate
blue bog stretching to a horizon
a four year old striding down a lane
the only witness a man digging.

His eye had drifted over me
then returned to his spade
the clean push of his heel
careful stacking of sods, smoke

soaked into his shirt, his fist,
his sweat, his straddle as he peed,
his caution -
of the sea, of trains, of travel.

We stand without landmarks
unable to push meaning
into stony outcrops
walk miles until we find a road.

Jane Kirwan

The Lady of Llyn y Fan Fach

There lived a widow by Mynydd Du,
    Her menfolk killed in battle,
Who sent each day her last own boy
    To the lake to mind her cattle.

One noontide as he prowled that shore
    Eating his barley bread
There danced at him from off the lake
    A sight that turned his head.

On the water's calm and glassy face,
    Combing her yellow hair,
Sat one whose dazzling loveliness
    Was a thing beyond compare.

This lady met his yearning gaze,
    He offered her his bread,
But gently she declined the gift
    And this is what she said:

'Put away your hard-baked bread,
    With that you'll win me never.'
Though straight she dived into the lake
    He swore he'd love her ever.

That night his mother bade him woo
    The maid with softer bread.
But the next day too she spurned his gift
    Though smilingly she said:

'Put away your soft-baked bread
    With that you'll catch me never.'
And as again she dived from him
    He wished her his forever.

Bread not too hard and not too soft
    Did his mother next advise,
And with it, at the lake next day,
    The farm boy won his prize.

'I'll dwell with you,' the maiden said,
    'And happy let us be,
But if with iron you strike me thrice
    You'll see no more of me.'

There burst then from the water's depths
    The father of the bride
Who dowried them with all the stock
    She could summon to her side.

'Remember, lad,' the old man said
    As the livestock streamed ashore,
'Three iron blows will drive all back
    To the lake for evermore.'

Three sons had they and happy years,
    He struck her ne'er a blow
'Til the day there was a christening
    To which she seemed loth to go.

'Hurry and fetch your mare,' said he,
    Flinging her bridle and bit.
'Ah!' cried she, as it struck her hand,
    'With iron you have me hit.'

The grief this first blow brought on them
    They edged in time aside,
'Til one day at a wedding feast
    Most piteously she cried.

'Hush!' he hissed as he flicked her arm
    With an iron-studded glove,
'Why weep you so untimely, wife,
    At a festival of love?'

'I weep,' said she, 'for bride and groom,
    And the sorrows that they'll see.
And you should weep, for twice 'tis now
    That iron has stricken me.'

The years passed by, their sons grew strong,
    And the fear he nigh forgot
That one more iron blow from him
    Would rend their good life's knot.

Then one day at a funeral
    With laughter she did flute.
To silence her he brushed her shin
    With his iron fettled boot.

'Such mirth when all is woe,' said he,
    I cannot comprehend.'
'I laugh,' said she, 'for when folk die
    Their woes are at an end.

'But your woes have just begun,
    From you I must depart:
Our marriage contract by this blow
    Is torn, o love, apart.'

Her stock she rallied to her side
    And like a harvest queen
She led them up towards the lake
    From yard and pastures green.

All followed, even a slaughtered calf
    And an ox-plough team of four,
All vanished then beneath the waves
    And were seen again no more.

Her searching sons no trace could find
    Of the lady's sudden leaving
Save, like a wound from farm to lake,
    A furrow steeply weaving.

Then one day she appeared to them
    As they thought they sought in vain,
And told them they should healers be
    To relieve mankind of pain.

She passed on to her family
    All the arts at her command,
And as doctors for generations they
    Were famed throughout the land.

Nigel Jenkins

The Broads

The Broads takes its name from the shallow lakes or broad areas of water formed from the flooded peat diggings of the medieval period. It is a landscape shaped by the history of the peoples that have sought to utilise its natural resources, and who were in their turn moulded by its nature.

Today, a journey through the Broads is still a poetic odyssey where pace and rhythm are measured in the steady flow of water through its enchanted landscape. Dense, tangled woodland gives way to open water and mysterious reed-fringed fen – where only a distantly viewed church tower or mill stands as a mute sentinel to humankind's enduring supplication to the vast canvas of an ever-changing sky. Its limits are framed only by those of the imagination. A haven for all manner of rare wildlife and plants, this unique, strange, wild and watery landscape has been an inspiration to artist, photographer, writer and poet, and a solace to all who venture into its quiet places.

In 1999 the Broads Authority celebrates the tenth anniversary of gaining status equivalent to a National Park. In that decade it has successfully striven to reconcile the interests of recreation, conservation and navigation, preserving the Broads for visitors and locals alike. In the words of Norfolk's great naturalist, Ted Ellis, it is, "a breathing space for the cure of souls".

Sam Bates, Information Assistant, Hoveton Information Centre (Norfolk Broads)

Norfolk

How did the Devil come? When first attack?
    These Norfolk lanes recall lost innocence,
The years fall off and find me walking back
    Dragging a stick along the wooden fence
Down this same path, where, forty years ago,
My father strolled behind me, calm and slow.

I used to fill my hand with sorrel seeds
    And shower him with them from the tops of stiles,
I used to butt my head into his tweeds
    To make him hurry down those languorous miles
Of ash and alder-shaded lanes, till here
Our moorings and the masthead would appear.

There after supper lit by lantern light
    Warm in the cabin I could lie secure
And hear against the polished sides at night
    The lap lap lapping of the weedy Bure,
A whispering and watery Norfolk sound
Telling of all the moonlit reeds around.

How did the Devil come? When first attack?
    The church is just the same, though now I know
Fowler of Louth restored it. Time, bring back
    The rapturous ignorance of long ago,
The peace, before the dreadful daylight starts,
Of unkept promises and broken hearts.

John Betjeman

From: *East Anglian Bathe*

How cold the bathe, how chattering cold the drying,
How welcoming the inland reeds appear,
The wood-smoke and the breakfast and the frying,
And your warm freshwater ripples, Horsey Mere.

John Betjeman

Peat-diggings in Winter

On rare occasions
The wind falls silent
And I on the bank,
Legs dangled over
Slow-hauled water,
Hear chinking mattocks
Chip fuel for a fire;

See in the mist
How a veil came down
To blur our view
Of the Middle Ages
So we were deluded –
Thought nature had fashioned
This Eden for us.

We're wiser now
And in Broadland winter,
Visitors gone,
When we are alone
With redshank and bittern,
The diggers return.
Listen. Listen.

Frances Nagle

From: *The Field, Tomorrow*

I wanted the bare field out there to be mine.
Each day, at my typing, I saw the smooth line
Of the sycamores, breaking the sweep of grass
To the farm and the river. I saw the sails pass
Far away, white and simple, where yachts moved
                          at Thurne.
And I looked down, in my pride, at my nearest stone urn.
From that urn to the sycamores, this was my land,
With the wide breadth of Norfolk stretched gold
                          on each hand.

George MacBeth

Cley Mill, Norfolk *(Ikon Imaging)*

Wroxham, Norfolk Broads *(Ikon Imaging)*

Horsey Mere, Norfolk Broads *(Ikon Imaging)*

The River Yare, Norfolk *(Ikon Imaging)*

Barton Broad

Light flies the bird in the air,
    Light runs the colt by the mere,
    Lighter still in the water clear
Are the swimmers there.

Still sits the swan on her nest,
    Still lies the fish in the deep.
    More silent yet our ship can sleep
On the water's breast.

Sunny the sea and the road,
    Starry the night will fall
    On the wild-fowl's haunting call
In the sheltered broad.

Fly high, run swift, swim light,
    Now is the moment of joy.
    For bird and for colt and for boy
'Tis the hour of delight.

Mary Gardner

The Deserted Aerodrome

Hangars are empty now; sea-slanted rains

Flood runways cracked with grass; partridge and gull,
Like forms of spitfires driven by the full
force of the wind fly over silent lanes.

Umbels of tansy gleam like beacons' light
Beckoning ground-safety; gaillardias shake
White, dropping parachutes, cloud-far, to make
From battlefield a naturalist's delight.

Well, they are gone, men and machines, more near
Intimates of death than soil or seed;
Now they are history who, for present need,
Emptied themselves of life and flew from here.

Mabel Ferrett

Broadland

The daylight fades, swift-scudding cloud
Swathing the waters as a shroud—
Sweeping far o'er the Broadland high
Rings many a mournful, eerie cry.

Across the sky-line's bar of grey
Pass flighting wildfowl on their way
To plunder, where deep dikes are free
With provender and sanctuary.

Downward, on graceful speeding wing,
Grey geese in level skein outswing
To distant space; and the echoes die
Away in a doleful lullaby.

Tense silence falls! Naught but the hoot
Of a lonely owl or straying coot
Seeking its mate 'neath the sedges hide
Abounding the osier beds divide.

A blinding sleet, and a grip that stings;
Again the flap of myriad wings—
Weathering the storm inland to seek
Shelter of some neighbouring creek.

Black night! The blizzard in fury rolls
O'er Broadland deeps, shallows, and pools.
No sound astir—save guns of war,
Grim sentinels of the North Sea shore.

Clarissa Alcock

"As the sun dapples the water ..."

The catalogue talks of reed-fringed rivers,
of wide open skies, windpumps and flowers.
It claims snipe and lapwing, even bittern.
Shiny pages portray pubs or museums,
and boats, so many boats.
The waters lap through grass and sedge.

A Danish king settled here and left his name;
wool-merchants their wealth and churches, a remote
and enigmatic place, religiously drained. Their houses
are hotels now; the staithes where reeds were loaded
harbour other boats – so many boats.
The waters seep through grass and sedge.

Tourists have found this haven. They come
in their thousands, seeking the tranquillity
denied at home. Skipper and Matelot, Cruiseliner,
Kingfishers without wings, each shreds the peace
it seeks – Boats, so many boats.
The waters surge through grass and sedge.

"A continual programme of upgrading
ensures all our boats have Colour TV, quality matching
china and portable phone ..." Comfort is assured,
for wide skies can chill, and starlight perturb those
more used to florescent strip. Boats, so many boats.
The waters rush through grass and sedge.

We begin to wear away what we love.
The bittern is almost silent. Nature Reserves
must preserve what was once common currency.
Yet who would deny the city dweller their two weeks
of longed-for peace – or their boats, though
their passage tears through grass and sedge?

Pauline Kirk

Dartmoor

Dartmoor is a distinctive and very special place of great scenic beauty and strong cultural identity. It is rich in wildlife and in reminders of our past – a place where people have lived for over 10,000 years, some 330 generations.

It is a land of variety and contrasts within itself and with places and life elsewhere, a visually stimulating land of patterns and mosaics, a land of sun, snow, mists, rain, wind, and of light shifts. Lichens and mosses clothe the trees and ancient rocks stand proud. It is a mysterious place where shapes loom out of the mist and where legends are made; a land of vast open spaces, dramatic valleys and native woods; a land where ponies freely roam and where rivers run clear.

Here is the largest piece of upland Britain to escape the scouring action of past glaciers, and here is a mix of habitats of national and international importance, including blanket bogs, upland heaths, wild rivers, grass moors, valley mires, and upland oakwoods. Such places provide homes for dormice, otters, red grouse and dunlin, for curlew, woodlark, buzzard and salmon, for golden plover and ring ouzel, for high brown fritillaries and blue ground beetles, bog orchids and heather.

Walking over Dartmoor we can cross not only vast physical distances but also time spans. We can trace its social and economic evolution from the fourth millennium BC to the present. Here is the best preserved, most complete upland archaeological landscape in north-west Europe comprising over 10,000 hectares of Bronze Age field systems and an extensive collection of ceremonial and funerary monuments. Here too are important medieval agricultural landscapes and relics of widespread industrial activity (particularly tin mining) going back at least 800 years.

Today, Dartmoor remains a living, working, dynamic environment – a land of farms but also a land of woods, watersheds and quarries where other traditional products of the land are gathered. It is an evolving place, yet here can be found timelessness, wild country, and remoteness from twentieth century phones, motorways, noise, pollution and crowds. It is a place to inspire writers, artists, sculptors, poets, composers, and a place to inspire us all.

John Weir, Head of Communications, Dartmoor National Park

Dartmoor: Stalldon Stone Row *(Carol Ballenger)*

Dartmoor: an inspiring combination of fields, woods and open moorland *(Ikon Imaging)*

Dartmoor: The Touchstone *(Carol Ballenger)*

New Year on Dartmoor

This is newness: every little tawdry
Obstacle glass-wrapped and peculiar,
Glinting and clinking in a saint's falsetto. Only you
Don't know what to make of the sudden slippiness,
The blind, white, awful, inaccessible slant.
There's no getting up it by the words you know.
No getting up by elephant or wheel or shoe.
We have only come to look. You are too new
To want the world in a glass hat.

Sylvia Plath

From: *Dartmoor*

... Then, rearward, in a slow review,
Fell Dartmoor's jagged lines;
Around were dross-heaps, red and blue,
Old shafts of gutted mines,
Impetuous currents copper-stained,
Wheels steam-urged with a roar,
Sluice-guiding grooves, strong works that stained
With freight of upheaved ore.
And then, the train, with shock on shock,
Swift rush and birth-scream dire,
Grew from the bosom of the rock,
And passed in noise and fire.
With brazen throb, with vital stroke,
It went, far heard, far seen,
Setting a track of shining smoke
Upon the pastoral green.
Then, bright drops, lodged in budding trees,
Were loosed in sudden showers,
Touched by the novel western breeze,
Friend of the backward flowers.

Coventry Patmore

Usurper Stone

Usurper stone,
You have taken the landscape
Under your command.
Upright, tall and slightly apart
From others' circles;
But then you always were.
Your triumph over the humble elements
Still sheers the lambkiller wind
And breaks the gnawing rain to tears.
This is your stone,
Not cut or hewn
But raised to its socket entire
As you knew it.
Huntress of the moon,
Did it hone your cutting edge?
Warrior queen, was it your platform
To rally the loyal to battle?
Woman, did it share your exploration
Of the private mystery of passion?

Your earthsign nearby
Now cups the mortal ground
At the focus of tors.
It holds me, still.
Sudden, strange pilgrims
Arrive unknowing, uncaring,
Drawn by curiosity
As they were before.
You take them as you took them then,
Usurper stone.

John Powls

Tor

Granite, grey
split
endless lines deep
a furrowed old face
that only nature alters.

John Weir

Solitude

Alone 'midst inspiring stillness
In the heart of the great wide moor,
Enrich'd with sunshine and shadows,
A fresh atmosphere, keen and pure.
The sigh of the wind through old stone walls,
And the curlew's haunting cry,
Above me the clouds, dazzling and white,
Drift over a rich blue sky.

Alone in this wondrous vastness,
Away from things that distract,
Resting 'mongst rocks, the bracken and gorse,
Forgetting life's ev'ryday facts...
The fairy-like mist, the wind and the rain,
Dew on the grass shining wet,
The first evening star, moonlight again,
Then dawn, sunrise, and sunset.

From Bellever's heights, great heart of the moor,
Communing with Nature – near Heaven's door.

Violet Francis

The Moor Grave

I LIE out here under a heather sod,
    A moor-stone at my head, the moor-winds play
        above.
I lie out here. . . . In graveyards of their God
    They would not bury desperate me who died for
        love!
I lie out here under the sun and moon;
    Across me bearded ponies stride, the curlews cry.
I have no little tombstone screed, no: "Soon
    To glory shall she rise!" – but deathless peace
        have I!

John Galsworthy

Small Talk at Wreyland

(in Memory of Cecil Torr)

It is hard to believe that he lived till the rise of the Nazis
And the General Strike and nine or ten Armistice Days
And that I was a child putting flowers on my grandmother's grave
Three churchyards away on the day that he died.

His forebears had gossiped their hold on the centuries.
One of them spotted Napoleon on the Bellerophon,
Moored in Torbay, with its prisoner slumping morosely
About on the deck; worldwide Boney, not looking his best.

Torr himself saw Garibaldi processing through London
As well as a Sultan, a King and two French elder statesmen,
But not half as plain as the Devil who hid in the bracken
Beside Yarner Wood, or a group of spiritual men
(As they used to call ghosts on the moors), or a stranger
Seen taking a little-known path to the top of a tor.

Never whimsical, even when speaking of saints like Sebastian
And Pancras who after their swim in the river of Paradise
Sat on a sunny bank drying their haloes.
He was sceptical; when the good men of Assisi
Described how St Francis knelt groaning in prayer all night long
He said with some reverence that Francis was probably snoring.
He was lazy himself except on his travels abroad.
He was cynical likewise: he felt that the clever embezzlers
And wayward but brilliant financiers imprisoned on Dartmoor
Might be asked to take over the work of his own District Council,
An honest but deeply incompetent body of men
Who had just spent five pounds on a signpost which got it all wrong,
Sending people to Wreyland instead of the station.

He watched Brunel's railway advancing (I watched it retreating)
Drumming its way up the valley from Newton to Moreton.
To begin with, his feelings were mixed, for it paid well and lured
The farm labourers out of their fields. But he came to enjoy it:
The evening train hooted on leaving the station
On its way to the plain, and the owls hooted back.
Engines had names and he met them all over the world.
He once saw Lars Porsena letting off steam outside Clusium.

The First World War seemed to mean little to him, being neither
Crimean nor Boer nor connected with Boney.
He scattered allusions: a boy who played tricks
On the spinsters of Lustleigh was killed in a battle, the name
Of which no one remembered; a wounded old friend of the author
Had married his nurse; on Armistice morning at Bovey
A flag had got stuck at half-mast after four years of killing.
He remarked that the prisoners-of-war in the neighbouring fields

Looked like the farmers' sons working beside them.
Well, they would, wouldn't they? Saxon blood, probably.
But he got angry about the Memorial, genteel and safe
Installed in the church, for he felt that the dead deserved granite
Somewhere up there on the tor which hung on to the light
Long after the Cleave was as dark and as wet as a trench.

Our paths almost crossed in the way that paths do on the moors.
He was interested in the name Beer and discussed it at length.
He believed it identified people who lived near a wood.
(In the days of surnaming it would have been difficult not to.)
My grandmother's people were natives of Chagford.
If she had not decided to go to Torquay
And enter good service, she might have been Cecil Torr's housemaid,
Streamering up to his room with a ewer of hot water.

He ended his small talk with thoughts of the little volcano
That long ago sneezed in what now is his parish, with dreams
Of a time when the soft parts of Dartmoor would sink in the sea
And the granite which held his house up in the air all those years
Would have turned into Wreyland, a reef on an up-to-date chart
Much respected by shipping and always made brilliant by waves.

I wish he could talk to me now that the day is declining
And the spiritual men are preparing to walk on the moors,
Talk about chimneys and highwaymen, talk about anything.
They say I have symptoms which can be controlled but not cured.
I am the same age as he was when chatting his way
Into darkness, his notions cavorting around him like fireflies.

Patricia Beer

The Ancient Stone Crosses of Dartmoor

In many a green and solemn place,
    Girt with the wild hills round,
The shadow of the Holy Cross,
    Yet sleepeth on the ground.

Richard John King

Princetown

In the town it seems just a local
Joke, like piskies or Uncle Tom Cobley,
Though in rather poor taste. Souvenir mugs
Insistent as fat-bottomed mums on seaside postcards,
And tiny priapic men: *Property*
Of HM Prison, Dartmoor.
Not to be taken away. But if you walk
The ripped-up railway, its stonework
The patient, perfect carving of cheap labour,
To the quarries, you begin to imagine
The bald, tanned pates, grotesque livery,
Automatic warders, routine hopelessness,
But far off, historic, like walking
The Roman Wall, reconstructing
A massive alert garrison from piles
Of rubbish. So here, until, nearing the town,
We saw the discreet bulk, shining in twilight,
Each window equally watted. And I remembered
The mother and daughter, arm in arm and crying,
Outside the café offering cream teas.

U.A. Fanthorpe

The Touchstone Inscription

Inspiring
This stone touching
Open moor and sky
Granite land mark
Raised to stand for
All times as one time;
Now, then and ever
In love and beauty
We are each other
Our story is a book
Always open
At the centre
Half of experiences
Half of un-named hopes.

John Powls

The Touchstone, from Dartmoor Prison quarry, was prepared and engraved by local artist/craftsman Kevin Andrews and raised in December 1999 on The Winter Solstice – see photographic section.

Standing on the Brink of Light

Half-finished monuments
By giant sculptors
The Dartmoor tors
Polished by sun's monocle-glint
Become shapes of fantasy
Points of reference
When shadow curtains
Draw slowly aside
To reveal green valleys
And purple-speckled plains.

Let one hand press rockflesh's
Immovability
The other finger dream of light
And, if you can do it,
In a moment of self-absence
Of deep concentration
Rock will turn back
To intricate fibres of old existence
And light transform
To pure points of meaning
Awaiting the surprise
Of the still persistent word.

William Oxley

Stephens' Grave, Dartmoor

(A Memorial Stone in Peter Tavy to a young local, John Stephens, who took his own life in October 1762, due to the unfaithfulness of his betrothed.)

I am playing cards again
With Jan Reynolds
In Widecombe Church.
To hell with the Devil.

Take it in slow motion.

Tread the same ground.

Walk through fists of cloud,
The granite bite of the air
Stinging your eyes.

Now you have it.

*

I try to claw my way
Back
To the same place,
A resonance in my skin

Like wind

Scraping

On dry stone.

But I cannot find you.

I howl through tolmens,
Screaming invocations,
Whisper dark words.

I am the tunnel man, the one who
Watches the cardiograph of the heavens,
Knowing
Their incendiary secrets.

Look for me
In the valley bottom woods,
In the rowan and hawthorn berry.

I'll come to you,
In winter, spring or summer.
I'll sing the same song.

*

Love! O love!
A terrible storm was raging then!
I went off, *Raven madness.*
I knew what I'd do.

Yesterday
I knocked the heads again
From the stone stumps at Langstone;
A celebration of power.

I went to Vixon Tor,
And wept for our love,
By the mutilated Egyptian Sphynx,
An old man now,
His back to the world.

How much
Did you think
This heart of mine could take?

This stark no nonsense grass
Is playing stunned,
Like the still woodland,
Bloodhead frozen,
As if some old deed
Said it must.

I have found my voice again
In a whinchat now.
I breathe
A bruised mist
Over the moor.

What I want most is you.
Your touch. Your kiss.
Not this.

Wendy Bardsley.

Legend has it that Jan Reynolds was carried off by the Devil for playing cards in Widecombe Church.

From: *Dartmoor, a Descriptive Poem*

Dartmoor! thou wert to me, in childhood's hour,
A wild and wond'rous region. Day by day,
Arose upon my youthful eye thy belt
Of hills mysterious, shadowy, clasping all
The green and cheerful landscape sweetly spread
Around my home, and with a stern delight
I gazed on thee. How often on the speech
Of the half-savage peasant have I hung,
To hear of rock-crown'd heights on which the cloud
For ever rests; and wilds stupendous, swept
By mightiest storms; — of glen, and gorge, and cliff
Terrific, beetling o'er the stone-strew'd vale;
And giant masses, by the midnight flash
Struck from the mountain's hissing brow, and hurl'd
Into the foaming torrent! And of forms
That rose amid the desert, rudely shaped
By superstition's hands when time was young;
And of the dead — the warrior-dead—who sleep
Beneath the hallow'd cairn! My native fields,
Though peerless, ceased to please. The flowery vale,
The breezy hill, the river, and the wood —
Island, reef, headland, and the circling sea,
Associated by the sportful hand
Of Nature, in a thousand views diverse —
Or grand, or lovely — to my roving eye
Display'd in vain their infinite of charms:
I thought on thy wild world, —to me a world, —
Mysterious Dartmoor, dimly seen, and priz'd
For being distant — and untrod; and still,
Where'er I wander'd — still, my wayward eye
Rested on thee!

N.T. Carrington

Dartmoor

The inner urges of the fell
are undone as the army
tests its artillery —
the wheatear plunges into rock
that should never
have been exposed to air,
the heather
fading

*

the gorse cap faintly bright
against the waste, black-faced sheep
with jaws exposed, stomachs hollowed
by foxes and buzzards
downwind
from the outlook, from granite tors
and stone settlements,
the horses being rounded up
for the locals' yearly
pound of flesh

*

the raven's nest fills the valley
as darkness leaks from the heath
nudging skewed and stunted rowan trees –
those haphazard solitaries
soon, a skylark will drop to sinkhole
where the rises fall towards
the fjord and the walkers
stumble forward
through the firing range,
the flags not up, the danger areas
and observation posts,
the solitary huts
of water-testers,
the massive inner swell
like blood petrified
and polished
by sharp winds

*

walkers huddle behind the Irishman's Wall,
thermos-flasks balanced in their laps,
compasses and maps growing damp
the animals dead quiet

John Kinsella

Exmoor

Possibly the least well-known of our National Parks, Exmoor still seems as if it holds secrets and its visitors feel that they have discovered their own special place. Its dense network of country lanes and tracks provide a sense of space in a small National Park. Such areas are, however, relatively large blocks of wild and unspoilt countryside and Exmoor is arguably, if not the wildest, the most unspoilt.

Much of Exmoor's character stems from its rocks, and the reds and greys of the sandstones and shales that permeate the landscape. Smoothly rounded hills and sea cliffs give a feeling of solidity whilst between them little combes give intimacy and a benign feeling to the moors. Tiny churches and small, isolated settlements reflect the traditionally sparse population of the moors yet historic remains show millennia of habitation in the same locations. The great changes of the Agrarian Revolution still show clear in the lattice of beech-topped earth banks that swathe the plateau between hilltops and valleys.

The moors and heaths come in infinite variety from the gaudy yellows and purples of the coastal heaths to the central moorland grasses, tinged with purple in summer and beige with the billowing broken leaves of winter. All are grazed by native wild ponies. Ancient woodland clings to cliffs and valleys where crooked oaks are festooned with lichens, ferns and mosses. In autumn they echo with the belling of rutting stags whilst mewing buzzards circle overhead.

Brian Pearce, Management Planning Officer, Exmoor National Park Authority

Exmoor Geometry

Arc of the moor's rim meets the sky's circumference,
One segment of its area is shaded black by summer fires.
Irregular quadrilaterals of pasture pave the adjacent valley,
Brown parallelograms of ploughland,
And dark rectangles of woodland.
Cubes of cottages and barns lie jumbled among them,
White and grey and rusty red.

On the moorland surface Man has drawn stone circles and
concentric rings,
Constructed the elliptical shapes of barrows
And the rough pyramids of cairns.
On the high ground his longstone drops a stark perpendicular.

Berta Lawrence

Culbone

Welsh saint Beuno climbed
The zigzag path from Porlock
Between oakwoods and the sea,
Raised his cell-church of wattle
Among trees and streams.
The bearded charcoal-burners
Sent up smoke between the oaks,
And in a lonely clearing
The outcast lepers lived
Cut off by the stream.

Poets walked here: talkative Coleridge,
Taciturn Wordsworth, wild-eyed Dorothy.
With Hazlitt the Shropshire lad,
And rustic Chester from Stowey.
Byron's daughter built her house.
Stately, Italianate.
Not a stone of it left,
Yet a little church stands
Among trees and streams.

Berta Lawrence

Naked Boy

(Naked Boy is a standing Stone inside the Exmoor National Park)

A winter's afternoon I came upon him,
Near the avenue of Brendon beeches
Naked as he, their creased old leaves discarded
And rustled by the wind. One way he looked
Through a field-gate at a flock of sheep,
Horned and black-faced, where he had seen the snipe
Drum up from the black bog, and then the labourers
Cutting long dykes and digging out the reeds.
Left, he looked at the old hill-trackway
Curling through teazles and hemp agrimony.
He had seen it running free, had seen
The bronze-smith tramp it, carrying his copper-cakes,
His casting-jets and bits of broken swords;
Watched a woman there, pulling meld by handfuls,
(And later, girls, picking violets and berries)
Saw the wolf come loping where these nights the fox
Trots swift and agile, and the badger shuffles.

The roar, the swish of motor-traffic breaks
The silence of his long-accustomed place.
Stubborn he stands and watches. So he watched
The horsemen and the waggons full of sheaves.
Soon, soon, they'll all be gone. He'll find himself
As solitary as when he came. Less naked
Though . . . Grey lichen and green moss will wrap
A few more rags about his nakedness.

Berta Lawrence

The Horses

I saw them once,
great Exmoor horses ploughing on Blackland Hill,
mouths foam-flecked, unblinkered,
manes flying free with the wind,
steady hands guiding them as they moved
slowly together across the skyline,
bright blades plunging deep into damp earth,
long furrows forming, ridge upon ridge,
thistles falling, the sun rising.
They did not see me standing there by the gate
watching them plodding the morning through,
nor wonder why I stayed so long,
they trod those stubbled acres patiently,
needing no angry voice or crack of whip,
until they came to rest, the sun high,
the ploughing done.

They are gone now, those beautiful creatures,
their day will never return;
the ploughman is dead.

I cannot forget them,
they stride all night through my country dreams,
I see them still at first cock-crow
in lanterned stables, waiting to be led out,
bells jingling, heads nodding,
to work those old fields again;
I hear the ploughman singing.

Leonard Clark

Cheriton Ridge

Yesterday on the ridge I saw two rooks
Earnestly mobbing a buzzard chick
Which perched ungainly in a stunted oak
Dressed in new green.

I reined and watched, my horse
Pricking his ears to the raucous voices
Of the merciless bullies.
And the new heather pushed through
The black swaled ground, as nature's
Unanswerable, uncomprehending springs unwound.

Tony Dunn

37

Exmoor

Exmoor Hunt pipe tobacco was the incongruous
Smoke favoured by my older friend, who sat
Surrounded by pictures collected in Prague,
Allowing himself an after-dinner puff
While Enid played Liszt on the Bosendorfer.
Exmoor would not have been Leslie's cup of tea.
(When his wife tried to seduce me, I resisted,
Not caring-much for women in trousers.)

But Coleridge's company he might have liked.
Having translated Hegel, he inclined
To speculation, and STC in spate
On the transcendental features of the sundew
(A plant I've seen kerb-crawling not far from Simonsbath)
Would have turned his mind to *Naturphilosophie*.
And a touch of sunburn had its appeal,
Connected in some way with youths in Sparta.

Without the two of them the world is barer,
The wind sighs over the moorland reservoirs
And sightless willows are delicately feeling
The faces of the water, wistful for features
That will tell them what all of us want to hear.
Way off to the west, beyond Lundy, stratified
Clouds with curling edges bar the sun –
And here comes the Exmoor Hunt (but not much cheering).

Fergus Allen

Exmoor Ponies on Exmoor *(Brian Pearce)*

Exmoor: Porlock Weir *(Brian Pearce)*

Exmoor: Woody Bay *(Brian Pearce)*

Exmoor: Culbone Church *(Brian Pearce)*

Kabla Khun

'the visionary dreariness' – Wordsworth, *The Prelude,* Book XI

The Person from Porlock was cooking his tea
    When Coleridge rapped on his door.
'Remember? You once did the same thing to me,
    Pimpled, Porlockian bore!'

The Porlockian seasoned his Somerset stew —
    'Oh, no, sir! The honour is mine!
A pleasure to be, sir, of service to you.
    Now, sir – some laudanum wine?'

'Pander to scales and a poet's addiction!
    You damned interrupter of dreams!
What-do *you* know of the still trance of fiction
    Half-written on opium's reams?'

'Ah, sir, but little, or nothing at all.
    I find what I like in Madeira.
After six draughts I'm stiff as a wall
    And my mirror reflects a chimera.'

The sky was a measureless laudanum-grey.
    It rose from an infinite sea,
Not Paradise milk, but a cloud-pewtered bay
    As real and undreamt as could be.

'Porlockian-pharmacist, how I love-hate you! -
    You sell me beginnings of vision.
Should I give you my hand, or roundly berate you,
    Or fetch you a kick of derision?

I've strolled through the lunar and ostracized city
    Down bat-lighted ginnels of Hell,
Heard pealing in Heaven carillons of pity
    Though truthlessness rang in each bell.

'From the zeniths of God to the bottomless pit
    Such pleasures, moon-sorrows, and pain!
Eternity, deserts, and seas, and an infinite
    Abstract, horizonless plain . . .

'Moments of magical foresight it gives me.
    On Wisdom itself it enthrones me.
My terrified mind howls for peace but forgives me.
    Sell me the substance that owns me!'

'Aye, queer stuff, they tell me, strange, mystical stuff
    That modifies vision and time.
One time and place, though, are never enough
    For poets who love the Sublime.

'Am I right? Am I wrong?' he said with a wink.
    In my youth, I, too, dabbled in verse.

In the night-time, I nibbed through whole potfuls of ink
    I *know* of that metrical curse.

It's heard in the scratch of the mineral pen
    Wrestling with words on the paper
When you fail to describe what you thought, yet again -
    My pen's an ignorant scraper.'

Anger shot forth from the eyes of Coleridge.
    He looked on the edge of despair
Or about to deliver English Romantic rage,
    As, roaring, he pulled at his hair.

'What are you? Who am I? And could it be true
    That the Person I need but detest
All along has been part of my being, and who
    Casts my shadow, interior guest?

'Where am I, and when? For my spirit is lost
    In the wrathfire of lies that I've told.
Ethical vagabond, in deserts of frost,
    I've been warmed where all fires are cold,

'Very cold Arctic blazes whose unmelting heat
    Releases its dancers of light
Whose movements describe all those whom I cheat
    In the ice and the salt of the night.'

I know that my substance inspires and destroys you,'
    The Porlockian mystery said.
I know how addiction grates and annoys you
    And how much you wish you were dead.

'But could it be true, that the meaning of you
    Depends on the meaning of *me?*
You chemical swillbowl, admit that it's true,
    And that you will never be free,

'Never, not ever, set free from your craving
    Distilled in the cauldron of mind,
Your Fancy, your Soul, and intelligence raving
    For Genius they might never find.'

'Please, don't condescend. You know who I am.
    You know what I do — but not *why,*
Said Coleridge, sipping his minstrelsy's dram.
    'So weigh what I want and I'll buy.'

His purchase was safe in his overcoat pocket.
    He set out for home in the dark.
His mind was his own, like a face in a locket.
    Each star was an audible spark.

His shoes in the puddles made visible splashes.
    Sights turned into sounds and sounds sights.
Cobwebby winds felt like God's own moustaches

And wrongs in the mind felt like rights.

Upside-down, inside-out, but astoundingly clear,
    He felt safe in the country called Mad
Where tomorrow is now and the far-back is near
    And good goes unchallenged by bad,

Where only the moon inhabits the present
    Along with the mind it possesses
In a city of stone composed of unpleasant
    Granite and maze-like addresses,

A city of staircases, handleless doors,
    Cul-de-sac tunnels and lanes,
Sinister engines, metaphysical floors,
    And you see someone else in the panes

Of the windows, expecting yourself — They're
                              unglazed! -
    And the noise is a grinding of clocks,
Going backwards, whose towers diminish, unraised
    By the levers of paradox.

This is my home. — Inverted Lucidity's
    Surrender to everything! Dreams!
Poetical minds must reach out for quiddities,
    Philosophical, crystal streams . . .

'For what lies beyond what we see, and beyond
    Dreary occasions, uselessly kind
Insights to social, familiar and fond
    Life that is known; it's the mind

'That's measured and placed by all metrical writing
    Weighing our time in the language.
It's the life of the self with another self fighting.
    I say this. Samuel Taylor Coleridge.'

He stood in a field off the road, in his city.
    It was raining and not very nice.
Rain on a hedge was a county of pity.
    I'm sorry for the sacrifice.

Douglas Dunn

Bagley Combe

I have come back to Bagley Combe.
This year mid-August the rowan is still ripening
and its neighbour may tree,
a greater presence than I remember,
has haws still raw.

Refreshing me from the sound of traffic,
the clear brown water rushes down
between banks where the long grass tangles
with deep gold birdsfoot trefoil,
splashes of purple heather, whortleberry
leaves beginning to blush,
reeds, thistles, cow parsley, interesting ferns.

I sit on soft sloping turf,
still dewy in places, with drops on little webs,
and dotted with rock roses' delicate yellow stars.
I try to avoid the rabbit droppings,
though they are dry and flaking back to earth.
Earth who basks in the morning sun
warming her bracken body hair,
that seems to exude her smell.

I lie still, belonging here
as just another life form she has grown.
I become part of the scenery.
Two rapid walkers –
speaking a North American dialect,
I wonder idly what tribe they are —
tramp down to the little ford,
over and up the other side
and do not notice me. I am glad.

Now I hear the grasshopper get busy
and all sorts of bird calls
I wish I understood.
This peaceful earth is energetic
with all her secret growth.
And peaceful here as part of her,
I rest at the heart of my life,
my purest energy, my most loving will.

All verbiage would break the silence,
the burdensome poundage of the Sunday papers,
even the prose I thought of producing
earlier this year, now seem too noisy.
But wording is part of my nature
and just as the grasshopper's chitter
and the stream rushing
increase the sense of repose,

my only recourse is poetry.
I invite it to visit me now
to stress and intensify.

The placard I carried recently –
Poets Support the Right to Silence –
was for justice,
against the Criminal Justice Bill.
And they danced in the fountains for liberty.
I have contributed so little
but out of the great silence
of the earth's eternal delight,
with all my will I want the promise kept:

For humanity not to fall short
of its poetry, the comfort
and pleasure it can imagine for everyone –
not just the gross and greedy few –
for the misery and waste to be over,
our whole species free to enjoy
the economy of its quiet earth,
obviously, naturally, as trees by water
whose clustering berries and haws turn red
when it's time, for the poem
the whole heart's reason resting here
cannot help raising – requiring an answer –
to become active, archway,
shimmering vista, word in deed.

So fellow creatures, when this large woman
outcrop of Exmoor landscape
comes home to London,
ruddy and weathered,
let me be building material.

Dinah Livingstone

Exmoor above Stoke Pero

On a brilliant day of soft billows
and a wash of multiple blues
I sit on a clump of whortleberries,
sample their half-sour dilution,
staining finger and thumb.
The young ling is fur on the flanks
downward to where the slope flattens,
flutters with various grasses,
wafts unfurling bracken sharp green
to me from as far as the line of beech.
On this ground I see cloud shadows passing,
an impermanent purpling,
as Moses from his hole in the rock
saw the back of the glory.

Amid monotonous bleating and mortal caws
over the steep meadow opposite,
where cows graze taking no notice,
these quiet shapes swifter than worship
keep up their stately procession,
ghosting the place, giant shades
coming and going impatiently,
while the combe cleft shaggy with scrub oak
is vulva seeming eternal
as the earth's curves, ample here
in intricate hills, full forms
shining, remaining,
inscaping the curls of the coast
mirrored in misty Wales across the water.

Dinah Livingstone

Exmoor

Winged stems glow through grey, burn with low flame
Against the grain of possessive rain, here's
Where sky and earth meet in spring's damp home,
Drips leaking from lead clouds over sodden acres.

Buzzards dip too, slip, dark pair, out of haze,
Grasp the still-stripped April limbs of trees:
Wet-cloaked usurpers of this kingdom of mist,
Wide heathered spaces where folk didn't last.

This wall stump's colonised by moss and root –
Stage for victors amid ruins of bracken.
We struggle with red mud, slipping back out
Past long-tongued ferns, stalks buckled and broken,

And clusters of gorse gripping lumpy grass,
Flickering on spiked stems where rough tracks cross.

Glyn Wright

From: *A Runnable Stag* (a famous Exmoor song)

When the pods went pop on the broom, green broom,
        And apples began to be golden-skinned,
We harboured a stag in the Priory combe,
And we feathered his trail up-wind, up-wind,
We feathered his trail up-wind —
        A stag of warrant, a stag, a stag,
        A runnable stag, a kingly crop,
        Brow, bay and tray and three on top,
        A stag, a runnable stag.

John Davidson

The Lake District

With 16 lakes and numerous tarns the Lake District is aptly named. The largest of England's National Park's, the Park offers 2.292 square kilometres of beautifully varying and contrasting landscape, consisting of high fells, rocky crags, lush green dales with long still lakes, vibrant villages and quiet hamlets. Here you can see England's highest mountain, Scafell Pike, and her deepest lake, Wastwater. You may also enjoy a look into literary legends such as that of William Wordsworth. The Park also has a coastal area on the West Coast from Drigg to Silecroft.

The National Park area has been the subject of much human activity, particularly farming, and people have been linked with the land for some 10,000 years. Here you can see stone circles, Roman forts, mediaeval monasteries, coppice woodland from the days of charcoal production for iron smelting, a stone wall pattern which mirrors the history of land enclosure and farms telling the story of what once was a thriving wool industry. More recent history is recorded in the spoil heaps of old mines, quarries and Victorian villas built for wealthy settlers.

In 1951 the Lake District was designated a National Park to protect its loveliness for future generations. The rocks beneath it vary from place to place along with its landscape. The fells to the north of Keswick for instance are smooth and moor-like compared to the rocky crags of central lakeland, and its southern lush rolling valleys similar to the nearby Yorkshire Dales.

In the 19th century the railways brought mass tourism here and such communities as Bowness, Windermere, Ambleside and Keswick blossomed to accommodate visitors. Today the Park's 42,000 residents live mainly from tourism, forestry, mining and agriculture. Upland sheep farming continues to shape the land and the hardy Herdwick sheep with their distinctive white faces and grey/brown wool are a common sight on the fells. The Lake District is also home to special plants and animals. The red squirrel, though under threat from the grey, its North American cousin, is still to be seen. Roe deer and a vast variety of bird life is also to be enjoyed. Birds of prey are a common sight on the fells, and on the lakes, coot, moorhens and ducks. Small fish called vendace, relics of the last Ice Age, are still to be found gliding in the waters of Bassenthwaite and Derwentwater, linking us with our past.

Emma Dewhurst, External Relations Manager, Lake District National Park

The Lake District: Scafell *(Ikon Imaging)*

The Lake District: Looking across
Windermere to the Coniston Fells
(Ikon Imaging)

The Lake
District:
Castlerigg
stone circle,
near Keswick
(Ikon Imaging)

The Lake
District:
springtime at
Sow How Tarn,
Cartmel Fell
*(Graham
Beech)*

Wordsworth's Umbrella

A parasol for the rain, large enough to accommodate
wet friends — De Quincey, Southey — or the household
women. Often it sheltered Dorothy as they walked
in lanes and fields of seeping hues:
the hilltops came and went under cloud,
water feeding the lakes, the lakes the land.

Lichen-coloured now, it's out of the damp,
a museum companion to the cloak and hat;
nearby, another record of lakeland days —
Coleridge's 'Ode to the Rain', in notebook hand.

I emerge again into insistent drizzle,
anoraked, watching the walkers in cagoules,
harsh colours against the subtle Grasmere greens.
That verdigree umbrella, giant fungus, blended
far better with this scene, aesthetic adjunct
to arthritic trees. I sneeze, reminded of Dorothy's
'Wm. slept ill. A soaking all-day rain';
of William's *'The rain came heavily and fell in floods'*;
and how she dried his hair before the peat fire
steadily glowing, the heart of their house place.
So powerful the link, the lakes seem theirs.

It recalls Ambleside, a honeymoon:
our future seemed as vast as Windermere
though misty at the edge;
in happy student poverty we walked
great lengths, wet fells, close under his umbrella —
our sole house place in those first days.
Since then, showers, monsoons:
the lakes absorb them and remain unchanged.
Returning now, I celebrate to find
an ancient umbrella and the same fine rain.

Gladys Mary Coles

Recollection of The Stone Circle near Keswick

(from *Hyperion*)

Scarce images of life, one here, one there,
Lay vast and edgeways, like a dismal cirque
Of Druid Stones, upon a forlorn moor,
When the chill rain begins at shut of even,
In dull November, and their chancel vault,
The Heaven itself, is blinded throughout night.
Each one kept shroud, nor to his neighbour gave
Or word, or look or action of despair.

John Keats

From a Boat at Coniston

I look into the lake (the lacquered water
Black with the sunset), watching my own face.
Tiny red-ribbed fishes swim
In and out of the nostrils, long-tongued weeds
Lick at the light that oozes down from the surface,
And bubbles rise from the eyes like aerated
Tears shed there in the element of mirrors.
My sight lengthens its focus; sees the sky
Laid level upon the glass, the loud
World of the wind and the map-making clouds and history
Squinting over the rim of the fell. The wind
lets on the water, paddling like a duck,
And face and cloud are grimaced out
In inch-deep wrinkles of the moving waves.
A blackbird clatters; alder leaves
Make mooring buoys for the water beetles.
I wait for the wind to drop, against hope
Hoping, and against the weather, yet to see
The water empty, the water full of itself,
Free of the sky and the cloud and free of me.

Norman Nicholson

Spring Images above Coniston

Still lake mirrors sky:
which is sky, which lake?

A clutch of toads tries sluggish limbs
on the clear bottom at the tarn's edge,
freezes at my footfall, shuffles stiffly
to the sanctuary of deep water.

Bluetits cling
to the tips of whippy branches,
swing like acrobats into the next tree,
applaud busily in loud whispers.

It's as bad as Market Street!
Stop for a second and some tramp,
got up like a chaffinch,
will accost you, tell you the tale,
beg a few crumbs or a bit of cheese.

A weeping willow,
a fountain of green leaves,
cascades in the sun.

A weasel, sly and furtive,
pauses on the path,
eye to the main chance,
slips me a look
appraising as a pickpocket's,
and writes me off.

Late snow on the Old Man's pate
and a muffler of white cloud.
He doesn't know it's a lost game —
already the mallards
have mated on the lake.

John Ward

The Walk

for Jan

This is as far from home as you can get,
back-of-Skiddaw's unspectacular fells
in the much-mapped, massively-written-about
walker's heaven of lark-sprung heathery hills

and falls. Dash Falls, for instance, doing away
with itself with revolutionary vigour.
And though he's long been lost to the light of day
you can still make out where that stooping, peaty figure

nicked and shovelled a small dark cliff of earth
some yards above the beck, backed up the horse,
took in the giant folio of the heath
and carried it off to long-lost Skiddaw House.

It's all but derelict now, the grove of larch
thrown down, in some old tempest, like Tai Ch'i,
root-tables torn aloft, pegged out to watch
a shower pass, the needles' slow decay.

Squat on a trunk, take in the broken star
of household glass, the stone shed on its back,
the soft, complicit turf, a clattery pair
of wingbeats, turning the silence in its lock.

William Scammell

Borrowdale in a Shower

(From: *Iteriad*)

The morning appeared with a great face of doubt,
Or to make us keep in, or to let us go out;
And at the first opening of joy-bringing dawn
Dark clouds of thick cloud round the mountain were drawn.
We look out of window, – call guides after guides, -
Demand whether rain or fair weather betides.
The first puts his thumb on one side of his nose,
And looks up to the smoke, to see how the wind blows;
Then pronounces it after a great deal of puffing,
"A vara bad dai! Whai, ye sees, sir, I'se can't hardly say;
Boot I'se think that it may be a middlin' fair day."
Another, – "For Skudda this never will do,
But I think's it prove fine, though not fit for a view;
And so if you liked it, a trip you might take
By Borrowdale, down into Boothermere lake."

John Ruskin (aged 11)

Skiddaw House

'The House was one of the loneliest dwelling-places in all the British Isles.' (Hugh Walpole)

Left for us to assume what purpose
it once had other than shelter;
remote in the bowl of hills behind Skiddaw
deep in its own decay; the peace stuns,
the filth accumulates, the questions gnaw.
How did anyone manage? Did they feed
on the shifting view of mountain tops?
Why put the windows facing north-east?
Some say it was for the shoot,
for nights away from the Big House
to be near the butts. Others that
it was given to shepherds
for weeks at a time, and they survived
because they knew there was somewhere else
nearer the auction and the ale.
Yet what if once it had been a family
living there, taking silver water from the beck
and setting off for a day's walk
to Keswick or Bassenthwaite.
Growing up taught by the hills' silence;
reading the shifting mist; working out God's pattern
from this piece of it. The larch coppice
smoothed into shape by the wind.
The gate into the four rows of vegetables
now on one hinge.

David Scott

Skiddaw and Derwentwater

And now I am a Cumbrian mountaineer;
    Their wintry garment of unsullied snow
The mountains have put on, the heavens are clear,
    And yon dark lake spreads silently below;
Who sees them only in their summer hour
Sees but their beauty half, and knows not half their power.

Robert Southey

The Ghostly Bells of Borrowdale

(From: *Christabel*, Part 2)

Each matin bell, the Baron saith,
Knells us back to a world of death,
These words Sir Leoline first said,
When he rose and found his lady dead:
These words Sir Leoline will say
Many a morn to his dying day.

And hence the custom and law began
That still at dawn the sacristan,
Who duly pulls the heavy bell
Five and forty beads must tell
Between each stroke – a warning knell,
Which not a soul can choose but hear
From Bratha Head to Wyndermere.

Saith Bracy the bard, So let it knell!
And let the drowsy sacristan
Still count as slowly as he can!
There is no lack of such, I ween,
As well fill up the space between.
In Langdale Pike and Witch's Lair,

And Dungeon-ghyll so foully rent
With ropes of rock and bells of air
Three sinful sexton's ghosts are pent,
Who all give back, one after t'other,
The death-note to their living brother;
And oft too, by the knell offended,
Just as their one! two! three! is ended,
The devil mocks the doleful tale
With a merry peal from Borodale.

Samuel Taylor Coleridge

Going Out from Ambleside

1

He is lying on his back watching a kestrel,
his head on the turf, hands under his neck,
warm air washing over his face,
and the sky clear blue where the kestrel hovers.

A person comes with a thermometer.
He watches a ceiling for three minutes.
The person leaves. He watches the kestrel again,
his head pressed back among the harebells.

2

Today he will go over to Langdale.
He springs lightly in his seven-league boots
around the side of Loughrigg
bouncing from rock to rock in the water-courses
evading slithery clumps of weed, skipping
like a sheep among the rushes
coursing along the curved path upward
through bracken, over turf to a knoll
and across it, around and on again
higher and higher, glowing with exaltation
up to where it all opens out.
That was easy. And it was just the beginning.

3

They bring him tea or soup.
He does not notice it. He is busy
identifying fungi in Skelghyll Wood,
comparing them with the pictures in his mind:
Purple Blewit, Yellow Prickle Fungus,
Puffball, Russula, two kinds of Boletus –
the right weather for them.
And what are these little pearly knobs
pressing up among the leaf-mould?
He treads carefully over damp grass,
patches of brilliant moss, pine-needles,
hoping for a Fly Agaric.
Scarlet catches his eye. But it was only
reddening leaves on a bramble.
And here's bracken, fully brown,
and acorns. It must be October.

4
What is this high wind coming,
leaves leaping from the trees to bite his face?
A storm. He should have noticed the signs.
But it doesn't matter. Ah, turn into it,
let the rain bite on the warm skin too.

5
Cold. Suddenly cold. Or hot.
A pain under his breastbone;
and his feet are bare. This is curious.

Someone comes with an injection.

6
They have brought Kurt Schwitters to see him,
a clumsy-looking man in a beret
asking for bits of stuff to make a collage.
Here, take my stamp-collection
and the letters my children wrote from school
and this photograph of my wife. She's dead now.
You are dead too, Kurt Schwitters.

7
This is a day for sailing, perhaps,
coming down from the fells to lake-level;
or for something gentler: for idling
with a fishing-line and listening to water;
or just for lying in a boat
on a summer evening in the lee of a shore
letting the wind steer, leaving the hull
to its own course, the waves to lap it along.

8
But where now suddenly? Dawn light,
peaks around him, shadowy and familiar,
tufts of mist over a tarn below.
Somehow he is higher than he intended;
and careless, giddy, running to the edge
and over it, straight down on splintery scree
leaning back on his boots, a ski-run
scattering chips of slate, a skid with no stopping
down through the brief mist and into the tarn.

9
Tomorrow perhaps he will think about Helvellyn ...

Fleur Adcock

Northumberland

Northumberland National Park is one of the most beautiful areas of England. At its core, the hills and moors are open and apparently empty: They give a glimpse of wilderness and solitude, a sense of harmony with nature which is rare and precious in our crowded island. This is "the land of the far horizon."

That man has touched this land lightly is, to an extent, an illusion. Few places in England can boast such a rich archaeological record spanning more than 7,000 years of occupation. This is also frontier territory in which the Hadrian's Wall complex and the bastle houses and pele towers from the turbulent Anglo-Scottish wars represent a unique built heritage.

The sense of continuity is also important. These are living landscapes with a community, largely still dependant on farming, with whom we must work and whose interests, activities and traditions we must respect. We value the collaboration with the Park community which we have enjoyed over the years and regard its continuation as absolutely essential to our task.

Graham Taylor, Chief Executive, Northumberland National Park Authority

Walltown Crags

This land was at the limits of a world
precariously picked out in stones,
regular as teeth, along the dolerite crags.
Long ago, its garrisons watched swans
on the dark lough, read omens in bog
and cotton grass, and when their time
was up melted like mist, their retreat
sounded by curlew and plover, world
and wall left desolate to wind
and moss and the indifferent rain.

John Ward

Northumberland

This is border country:
memories are long.

Only yesterday,
on moonlit nights,
reivers drove cattle
north up these roads,
left at their backs
cut throats,
burning homesteads.

Listen at evening
in Branxton field.
Listen well.
Above the curlews' song:
hiss of flying arrows,
agony of horses,
screams of dying men.

John Ward

Branxton field was the scene of the Battle of Flodden, 1513

Recent History

Having filled the space
Between the event
And its recollection
With an album of feathers

Found in a birdless city,
Hadrian left Antioch
Trailing the exclamatory
Quills of magpies.

Architecture is politics
By other means,
He thought, and saw,
In the structure of feathers,

A possible future
For buildings – slim towers
With floors pinioned
On a single hollow stem

With syphon-powered
Paternosters. And further,
Feathers themselves as
The supreme building material –

Downy courts, pillowy piazzas,
Fluffy, snug palaces and theatres
Vapid, deep, cosy,
With walls full of give ...

This in a man so concerned
With outlines. He defined
The empire with a fringe
Of limestone, ancestor

Of plumage. He saw it
As a massive wall of feathers,
Blown away on Pictish breezes,
Reappearing, much later, as history.

Gerard Woodward

Routing Linn, Northumberland

(for Sid Chaplin)

Tucked out of sight of the Cheviot massif,
the site itself was convenient
for defence: to south and west
a deep-wooded gorge echoing with the Celts'
bellowing cataract – even withered
to a trickle, the noise seems to hiss through the copse,
overflowing birdsong and the easing
of wind through trees across the scarp.
To north and east four giant ramparts and ditches
grooved in an arc still reek of man
through the dry March bracken and rampant
shrubbery. Blackbirds and throstles cluck off
in pairs, an affronted cock pheasant
squawks upwards in a russet feathering of alarm,
glinting red and green.
Picnic litter flakes the grass.
On the edge of the road a dead mole bares
its pale-furred belly to the sky's predators.
At the edge of the camp
there's a massive grey sandstone boulder
as if frozen at a point
where it has not quite freed itself
from peaty earth and last year's ling.
It is studded with sculptured signs
all but erased by the precipitation
of perhaps three thousand years: time and man
co-operators of this alien delicacy,
these hermetic markings that fuel
our hermeneutic urge.
Most are concentric rings centred by cup-holes,
chipped out by stone or bronze, roughly tooled,
often with a downward extended radius
like soaring ideograms of a comet.
Some, plainly, are ripples of rain falling
in a pool of stone.
Other carvings; overturned U-shapes
stacked on top of each other,
primitive stalk and flower forms, as full of grace
as a passionate hope, yet arcane
as the roots of worship.
Some could be signs of one-eyed death
or the lapidary emblems of life-force,
reverberating planets and analogues of divinity;
fertile tree-rings, patternings of birth
or sacrifice, or prosaic maps of *oppida*. They mingle

familially with natural hieroglyphs,
and give to elemental groovings and groins of rock
where rain stagnates
and to the cavities and quarry-traces
of later farmers, a sense of latent design.
After so many centuries their purpose
seems immanent in the stone, but secretly larval.
They might be symbols of transmigrating souls,
as Berwick naturalists thought a hundred years ago,
or metaphors of the flux of blood and time,
to placate the supernatural.
They might.
They offer a meaning that is imagistic
yet obscurely discursive: imponderable
echoes rippling in the mind. The fading
beauty of their bas-relief excites
seductive dreams of ancestral mysticism – why not
say only that such signs are there still
to strike a spark
in imaginations that hold a streak of flinty reasoning?

Rodney Pybus

On Hadrian's Wall

This shield is no defence against the gale
which is a wind I do not recognize.
It comes from places where we fear to go:
where hillsides wild with trees hide wilder men
than any we have known. Their knives are sharp
and every word they speak scrapes at their throats
and makes us flinch, as if it were a stone
thrown from the mouth in anger. Thrown at us.

When I stand here, I think myself away,
conjure the sun somewhere inside my head
and pull my cloak around me. And my eyes
fall on an emptiness of moor and fell.
The metal sky seems close enough to touch
and horizontal rain stabs at my face.
The smell of lemons. Cypress trees. Blue sky.
I concentrate on those and pace the wall.

Adèle Geras

The Journey

As I went over fossil hill
I gathered up small jointed stones,
And I remembered the archaic sea
Where once these pebbles were my bones.

As I walked on the Roman wall
The wind blew southward from the pole.
Oh I have been that violence hurled
Against the ramparts of the world.

At nightfall in an empty kirk
I felt the fear of all my deaths:
Shapes I had seen with animal eyes
Crowded the dark with mysteries.

I stood beside a tumbling beck
Where thistles grew upon a mound
That many a day had been my home,
Where now my heart rots in the ground.

I was the trout that haunts the pool,
The shadowy presence of the stream.
Of many many lives I leave
The scattered bone and broken wing.

I was the dying animal
Whose cold eye closes on a jagged thorn,
Whose carcass soon is choked with moss,
Whose skull is hidden by the fern.

My footprints sink in shifting sand
And barley-fields have drunk my blood,
My wisdom traced the spiral of a shell,
My labour raised a cairn upon a fell.

Far I have come and far must go,
In many a grave my sorrow lies,
But always from dead fingers grow
Flowers that I bless with living eyes.

Kathleen Raine

Poem found at Chesters Museum, Hadrian's Wall

To Jove, best and greatest
and to the other immortal gods;
to Augustus, happy and unconquered
Victory, holding a palm branch;
to Hadrian
commemorating 343 paces of the Roman Wall

> *bill hook, holdfast, trivet*
> *latch lifter, nail lifter, snaffle bit*
> *sickle blade, terret ring, spear butt*
> *boat hook, entrenching tool*
> *chisel, gouge, gimlet, punch*

To Longinus, trumpeter
and Milenus, standard bearer
1st Cohort of the Batavians;
to Cornelius Victor
served in the army 26 years
lived 55 years 11 days
erected by his wife;
to Brigomaglos, a Christian;
to my wife Aelia Comindus
who died aged 32

> *unguentaria*
> *balsamaria*
> *ivory comb*
> *pins of bronze and bone*
> *dress fastener*
> *strap fastener*
> *spinning whorls*
> *needles, spoons*
> *Millefiori beads*
> *ligula, earprobe*
> *tongs*

To the woodland god Cocidius;
to Coventina, water goddess
and attendant nymphs

> *—in her well*
> *axe hammer*
> *spiral ring, jet ring*
> *dogbrooch, coins*

To the Mother Goddesses
to the gods of this place
to the goddesses across the water
to the old gods
to a god ...

dedication partly obliterated
with human figure in rude relief
text of doubtful meaning
dedication illegible

uninscribed

stone of ...

Frances Horovitz

The Roman Wall

Though moss and lichen crawl
    These square-set stones still keep their serried ranks
Guarding the ancient wall,
    That whitlow-grass with lively silver pranks.

Time they could not keep back
    More than the wind that from the snow-streaked north
Taking the air for track
    Flows lightly over to the south shires forth.

Each stone might be a cist
    Where memory sleeps in dust and nothing tells
More than the silent mist
    That smokes along the heather-blackened fells.

Twitching its ears as pink
    As blushing scallops loved by Romans once
A lamb leaps to its drink
    And, as the quavering cry breaks on the stones,

Time like a leaf down-drops
    And pacing by the stars and thorn-trees' sough
A Roman sentry stops
    And hears the water lapping on Crag Lough.

Andrew Young

Lindisfarne Priory off the Northumberland coast – an Area of Outstanding Natural Beauty just a few miles from the boundary of the Northumberland National Park *(David Burton)*

Northumberland National Park:
Hadrian's Wall, looking east from
Housesteads Roman fort *(Ikon Imaging)*

St Cuthbert's Way runs from Melrose to Lindisfarne, climbing the hills around Kirk Yetholm (right) in the Scottish Borders before passing through the hamlet of Hethpool (below) in the Northumberland National Park. *(Graham Beech)*

Rebuilding a Dry Stone Wall

She saw new light smooth his forehead,
the crests and edges of the stunted wall,
the boulders at its feet, their facets
gleaming from the quiet grass. The ball

of his hammer formed an arch around her,
drew her in, while she eased the stones
to view, arranged them at his feet
like pearls. He saw the filigree of bones

beneath her blouse. Her eyes were averted
from the hills. Throughout the day he weighed
the stones, upheld their line, slid shards
of slate to level them. At noon he laid

the ones he'd saved to make a heart,
in lichen, on the wall. As its shadow crept
towards the fields his rhythm grew perfect,
strong. He, Hadrian, rode chariots, leapt

fords, split skulls with cunning taps.
He did not see her kneeling, slow tears
splashing on the proferred stone, pressing
it gently to the ground. Round the years

of their youth she drew a circle. She turned
towards the hills. It reached its height
at dusk. He stood bewildered by the boulders
lying at his feet. He roared into the night.

John Latham

Cheviot Autumn

Sunlight, a philosopher's stone,
turns October chestnut and rowan,

ablaze, into golden torches,
transmutes guinea-yellow beaches,

sucks opulence from withering
bracken on Harthope and Yeavering,

bestows its last slow benediction and peace
on old men, flat-capped in market place.

Shadows lengthen, pale, over stubble-gold.
Soon to be over. The rest, winter will geld.

John Ward

The North York Moors

Striding across open moorland, wind in your hair, heather beneath your feet is the image most people conjure up of the North York Moors. Yet, this lovely area of northern England is a place of contrasts; a wonderful mosaic of intimate villages, spectacular coast, ancient woodland, lush farmed dales and of course beautiful heather moorland.

The North York Moors is an upland plateau bounded by the Vale of Pickering to the south, Vales of York and Mowbray to the west and the River Tees to the north. Its eastern edge is the dramatic North Yorkshire and Cleveland Heritage Coast; 36 miles of rugged cliffs, sandy beaches, bays and headlands. The landscape, the weather and the sea have given the coast a character and culture all of its own. Tiny villages nestling beneath the cliffs have provided shelter for fishing boats, easy getaway for smugglers and a welcome to artists and writers who have come to gain inspiration from the changing moods of the coast.

The moors and dales, too, have a unique quality, one not easily defined but one which visitors who come again and again have discovered. Although magnificent when the heather is in flower, for much of the year, the moorland is bleak. But it is the bleakness that has shaped the nature of the place. It offers a sense of freedom, where you can see the horizon and man, so it seems, does not intrude. The dales, though, are a striking contrast, a patchwork of drystone walls, small fields, woodlands, farms and picturesque villages. They offer the soft and welcoming face of the North York Moors.

Like all the National Parks in England and Wales, the North York Moors is undoubtedly a very special place where man and nature together have created a landscape to care for and a place to enjoy.

Jill Renney, Project Manager, Countryside Interpretation and Information Services, North York Moors National Park Authority

A Lyke-Wake Dirge

This ae nighte, this ae nighte,
 —Every nighte and alle,
Fire and fleet and candle-lighte,
 And Christe receive thy saule,

When thou from hence away art past,
 —Every nighte and alle
To Whinny-muir thou com'st at last;
 And Christe receive thy saule.

If ever thou gavest hosen and shoon,
 —Every nighte and alle,
Sit thee down and put them on;
 And Christe receive thy saule.

If hosen and shoon thou ne'er gav'st nane
 —Every nighte and alle,
The whinnies sall prick thee to the bare bane;
 And Christe receive thy saule.

From Whinny-muir when thou may'st pass,
 —Every nighte and alle,
To Brig o' Dread thou com'st at last;
 And Christe receive thy saule.

If ever thou gavest meat or drink,
 —Every nighte and alle,
The fire sall never make thee shrink;
 And Christe receive thy saule.

If meat or drink thou ne'er gav'st nane,
 —Every nighte and alle,
The fire will burn thee to the bare bane;
 And Christe receive thy saule.

This ae nighte, this ae nighte,
 —Every nighte and alle,
Fire and fleet and candle-lighte,
 And Christe receive thy saule.

Anonymous

Whinnies = gorse

The Moors

Here nature is barely sketched out
    All is a threadbare mat of grass,
    Brutal rock, the dark-wet gash
    Of peat, the call of peewit and lark's far shout —
A place where under thin stretched sky
A man may walk and wonder how he'll die.

    Here where the savaged or mis-born
    Lamb rots by a shedding burn
    Or the wild crow dies in the sun
    Is the graveyard of aestheticism.
Moors are not for the squeamish or lonely
They are the playground of the solitary.

    Theirs is a proud drabness of flint and stone
    Where grass is tough as wire
    And the winded rocks ache like old bones.
    Deserted they do not invite much growth:
Man and history would pass them by the while;
Yet in legend and question they're strangely fertile.

William Oxley

Gorse

Gorse denies the season's bleakness
Even in December's fret.

Gorse is always blooming somewhere –
Not in summer's heaps which burn

But round a corner, in a fall
Of water meeting water, find

That spike of flame inside the green
Surprising for its littleness,

That brimstone tip of kindling
Which reawakens everything —

'When the gorse is in bloom
The kissing is in season.'

Peter Morgan

Staithes Song

From Eight Bells and Gun Gutter
Broom Hill and Lining Garth
Beck Side and Laverick Doorstones
Old Stubble to Barber's Yard
Up Slippery Hill to the Barras
Through Dog Loup up from the Staithe
The fret's creeping in from the harbour
As the tide brings it on the wave

Safe and calm, safe from harm
In the warm embrace
Cowbar Nab, Penny Nab, Those two strong arms.
Up top, down Steers, where you will
Rolling Cross is standing, Rolling Cross is standing
Rolling Cross, Rolling Cross is standing still

'Love Divine' and 'All My Sons'
A-sailing in the morning
'Seaton Rose' and 'Golden Crown'
Hiding from the storm
'Coronation Queen' and 'Star of Hope'
Guided by the brave
The fret's creeping in from the harbour
As the tide brings it on the wave

Safe and calm, safe from harm
In the warm embrace
Cowbar Nab, Penny Nab, Those two strong arms.
Up top, down Steers, where you will
Rolling Cross is standing, Rolling Cross is standing
Rolling Cross, Rolling Cross is standing still

Oyster catchers, herring gulls
Circling in the twilight
Postcards and photographs
Fading in the dawn
Memory and history
Souvenirs to save
The fret's creeping in from the harbour

Safe and calm, safe from harm
In the warm embrace
Cowbar Nab, Penny Nab, Those two strong arms.
Up top, down Steers, where you will
Rolling Cross is standing, Rolling Cross is standing
Rolling Cross, Rolling Cross is standing still

Written in 1999 by the people of Staithes during the project 'Making Waves' which was funded by the North Yorkshire and Cleveland Heritage Coast Project, the North York Moors National Park and the Countryside Agency, and facilitated by Jim Woodland of Blaize.

Robin Hood's Bay

I've sailed the world over
    Seen towns of all nations
Old England at times
    I haye been through and through
In search of a ship,
    Or to see my relations,
For sure Jimmy Jenkins
    Is known to a few.

And oft must I own
    Have my eyes been delighted
To view the rich splendour
    Proud art can display
But never a spot, though
    The place may be slighted,
Can equal the charms
    Of sweet Robin Hood's Bay.

It was there I was born,
    Spent the years of my childhood,
And thought my lot hard
    To be subject to rule
And often I've pondered
    While roaming the wild wood
Upon the cruel folk
    Who invented the school.

But grandmother's gone
    And her dwelling is shattered
The school house is hastening
    Fast to decay.
The comrades who shared
    In my pleasures are scattered
Save five who remain
    In sweet Robin Hood's Bay.

In my good ship the 'Beulah'
    Across the wide ocean
To foreign lands oft
    Was I summoned away
Then I published aloud,
    This you'll think a strange notion,
The romantic beauties
    Of Robin Hood's Bay.

One day in Calcutta
   Alone I was walking,
A Nabob, or King,
   Bade me tell of my land
And as of its beauties
   I freely was speaking
In rapture he answered:
   'Your country is grand
But where shall I find
   With a suitable dwelling
The name of your city?
   Come tell me I pray,
 I answered, 'Across the blue waves
   That are swelling
You'll find the famed city
   Of Robin Hood's Bay.'

Anonymous c1840

The name Robin Hood's Bay does not appear in any records until Tudor times. Leland, visiting in 1538, described the village as, 'A fischer tounlet of twenty bootes caullid Robyn Huddes Bay, a dok or bosom a mile yn length.'

Robin Hood is supposed to have lived in the 13th century and there is no evidence to connect the outlaw with Robin Hood's Bay. Canon Atkinson of Danby, author of *Forty Years in a Moorland Parish* (Macmillan, 1907), considered that the ancient forest elf 'Robin Hood', a spirit creature something akin to 'Robin Goodfellow', was the more probable origin of the place-name. The barrows on the moor above the bay were said to be haunted by him.

Another visitor, Mrs Louise Chandler Moulton, writing in her *Lazy Tours* (Ward Lock, 1896), described the place as, 'The strangest village it has ever been my fortune to behold.'

Between the Heather and the Sea

Between the heather and the sea
A slipshod curve of arable and scree
Climbs from the sea to seeping moor
Where in between the neighbourly
And not so neighbourly close doors
Against the winter wind, the sleet,
The dull necessity of speech.

Peter Morgan

Roots In Lastingham

Twelve centuries ago the Venerable Bede
looked with misgiving on the lonely place.
Its craggy and distant hills, he wrote,
were like the lairs of robbers and wild beasts.
The habitation where dragons dwelt must be cleansed
by prayer and fasting, and a monastery built in stone.

The work was well done. The purple heather
and the sharp apple-green of bracken-shoots
conceal no foes. My Quaker forbears farmed
unharmed two hundred years their Bankfoot freehold,
coaxed a living out of sheep on Spaunton Moor
and corn in the hollow sheltered by the hills.

They are gone. No guarantee of immortality lay
in all those souls born to each succeeding generation.
The land was finite. Their excess went into exile
and left its dust in the Australian outback,
the veldt, in Pittsburgh, New York, and nearer home
in Cleveland mines and half North Riding's towns.

The anchor-man, our earliest root, lies safe,
immune from change in Lastingham churchyard.
His lichened stone in deep yew-shadow reads:
John Ward interred here November nineteenth
seventeen-fifty-nine aged sixty years.
No wasted words, no useless eulogies.

As simple in their way as ever Bede,
they sent him to his God in working dress.
I feel close: kinsman, namesake, ancestor,
planted in death in soil you worked alive.
My fingers stretch, touch gently your rough stone.
Nowhere as fitting will embrace my bones.

John Ward

Robin Hood's Bay from Ravenscar (*Photograph courtesy of North York Moors National Park*)

The North York Moors: Cleveland Hills, near Bilsdale *(Ikon Imaging)*

North York Moors: Staithes (*Photograph courtesy of North York Moors National Park*)

From: *Lealholm Bridge*

(A soliloquy during a visit, after some years' absence.)

Ah, lovely Lealholm! where shall I begin,
To say what thou art now, and once hast been?
Once the dear seat of all my earthly joys,
That now, in recollection only, rise!
    Methinks, where'er I look no life appears,
But all the place a cheerless aspect wears;
Thy groves are desolate, thy swains are fled,
And many of them numbered with the dead;
Religion's cold, the poor are sore oppress'd,
Thy orphan's weep, and widows are distress'd.
O let us pray their griefs may shortly end,
And God, their Father, still may prove their friend.
    This ancient bridge some feint idea brings,
Where still the swallow comes and dips her wings;
The murmuring river, and the rumbling mill,
Bear some resemblance to poor Lealholm still;
Yon silent whirlpool beautifies the scene,
Where shadows of trees are in its deepness seen;
Where leaping fishes on the surface play,
And gladly seems to close the summer's day;
The broken waters from yon glen resound,
Their constant ripling's heard the village round.

John Castillo – The Bard of the Dales (c1850)

Lowna Burial Ground

1

This is the place of pilgrimage,
my pit and rock, my psychic pole.
A plaque in the stone wall proclaims:
'Between the years 1675 and 1837
there were buried here 114 Friends.'
My family's share was eight or ten.
The small enclosure is scattered
with fragments of our story.

Anonymity suits. Its simplicity confirms
the courage of their modest lives.
They went into the dark without display
or intercessionary praise of marbled words,
allowed no jack in the steeplehouse
to plead their cause. They would say
what had to be said, face to face
like honest men, or hold their peace.
(I doubt when my time comes I shall do half as well.)

2

No sign of their interment disorders
cropped grass or shrivelled leaf,
but the silence seems full of strictures
and something I cannot see is watching me.
Its long one-sided scrutiny disturbs.
I fumble for the right emotion, conscious
that a nineteen-seventies man cannot say:
'At last, I have come to show myself,
to acknowledge you in the proper place,
to discharge the debt of my inheritance.'
Too much of their Dissenting blood is mine
to form such words without embarrassment.
And yet, if not that, what else
has brought me to their burial-ground?

3

The sanctuary has filled with shadow,
an evening redolent with peace,
and it is time to go.
                    Stumbling over stones,
I mind those brethren, scolded in Meeting,
whose heart quailed at the two-mile carry,
uphill most of the way, rough underfoot,
who felt the need of stronger drink
and richer meat than some approved
and cared less for a punctual journey's end

72

than purists waiting under trees,
fretting after better days when men kept time.

My spirit is consoled;
their weakness keeps mine company.
It is easier to walk with sinners than with saints,
the debt to be discharged is that much less.

John Ward

Goathland School c1880

Yes! There are ghosts!

Haunting neither hall, nor castle,
they walk the mind's streets
with silent tread, present
when we are least aware of them.

Shadows that dance around
the sundial's gnomon, moving
towards high noon
when the dandelion seeds
spatter the grass and grow.

This small picture,
hand-painted, sepia
with age, of a Goathland school:
the name of the schoolmaster –
remembered: Michael Frankland.

He left a scattering
of poems and stories:
my inheritance.
So, I come to Goathland
seeking my roots:

seeking a vanished classroom,
a vanished hand;
threading needles of memory
that I only, I alone,
have possession of – now.

Mabel Ferrett

Kleptomaniac

The Park's coastline from Boulby Cliffs in the north through to Long Nab in the south is fast collapsing into the sea. Old, and not so old, maps reveal names of villages that no longer exist. The Jurassic sandstone and shale and glacial boulder clay is easy prey for the fierce equinoctial tides.

The sea has set its stalls
Halfway along the beach.
We rummage through its bric-a-brac,
Collect smoothed glass, driftwood,
Unusual rusty shapes.

Snatched down from someone's roof,
Sucked cornerless,
A marled and sooty stack
Sunk into the sand.
Who would have thought to find this here,
Brick-red symbol of the heart of home?
And close by,
A whole corner of a house,
Claimed and prised away
As frightened fingers lost their grip.

Were they prepared,
The family on the sofa by the fire?
It was a familiar sound,
The hungry sea opening wide its jaws,
Calling down on the tongue of the wind
Into the room. Tweaking the lights.

Generations had heard it so.
Slept with it. When angry,
Bellowed at each other over the top of it,
Were drowned out and laughed.
The storms come closer they said,
Kept saying.
Only the gardens shivered and shrunk.

Imagine that sea,
Gnashing and grinding and hissing,
A great, greedy cobble-filled mouth,
World traveller in league with the wind,
Defining and looting the land.

Then that house, a home,
Raked down on a whim
To end gobbed at the clay cliff's back
With spittle and trash from the sea.

A kleptomaniac is stamping down this coast
Shouting *I WANT! I WANT!*

Pat Borthwick

Realising that the World is Round on the North Yorkshire Moors

All I remember
is that Auntie Mary and Uncle Jack
had walked away that way

looking for Josephine and our John,
and my mam and dad
had been over there, getting the stove going

by the golf balls that would warn us
of Martians or Russians
and I had looked at Uncle Jack's head

lowering, lowering, as he walked
to the place where the sky brushed
the moor's cuff

and I couldn't see Auntie Mary
because she was smaller
and it was a moment of physics,

pure physics. The world was round.
If it had been flat, Uncle Jack's head
would not have lowered like that,

Auntie Mary would have been
completely visible all the time.
Physics. Moor physics.

Ian McMillan

The Peak District

The Peak District National Park is the second most visited national park in the world after Mount Fuji in Japan. It was also the first in Britain, designated nearly 50 years ago in 1951. Visitors have been drawn for centuries to the "Wonders of the Peak" and those visiting Chatsworth or the Blue John caves at Castleton today are following early travellers such as Daniel Defoe and William Wordsworth.

The Park has two sides to its character: the deep, dramatic dales of the White Peak; and the wild, high moors of the Dark Peak. A glance at the field walls explains the difference. The White Peak has light-grey carboniferous limestone, packed with fossils, as its underlying geology. The Dark Peak is millstone grit – a stone which weathers to a sombre dark grey.

Dovedale, popularised in the 17th century by the writer Charles Cotton, is the best loved of the limestone dales and still has its quick, clear water and famous stepping stones. Further north, Edale in the Dark Peak is the start of the Pennine Way. On the high flat summits of Kinder and Bleaklow you will have only sky and the golden plover's plaintive *wheep, wheep* for company. The world below is out of view and could be a million miles away.

John Sewell, Historic Building Architect, Peak District National Park Authority

Stone-walling

I

Looking down, across and beyond from Roach End
apart from the everywhere greenness of bracken frond
of trees clinging to the valley
and, up above, the fielded grass
notice the walling imposing a net on the land.

It forces its presence
has been around so long seems indigenous
is difficult to imagine otherwise.

The land has been encompassed, its flight ringed.
But the mind cannot comprehend such engineering.
There's so much of it
so unspectacular yet so vast
put end to end where would it stretch?

Incalculable the many millions of stones.
Even the Pyramids cannot match this mammoth task.

(Today we take so much for granted,
question little that happens outside our home.
Imagination's a commodity that's not wanted.)

II

They must have worked to a ground plan
those huge, yet still mean, men labouring away
those moorlands-poor building a living
in field after field, hillside on hillside
how else did they know they'd end where they began?

Piling stone on stone, packing with flats, the chipped bits
to make calendars of the past for the future
stretching before them, reaching back and out behind them.
Such patience a penance.

And the carting, the quiet straining horses
the lugging, and lifting, the hauling maul
the dressing-chisels clipping out messages of possession
so much sweat's worth under the broiling sun.

And after work
the bent spines, torn hands, grit-scraped skin.
Such humble offerings.

They might have hoped it would last so long
two centuries and more
or was it to be forever
the monumental permanence never to fall down?

All for your forefathers, you soddy blank-eyed scraggy sheep
bleating out at trespassers, curved curlews and errant clouds.

III
How many hernias did your sort cause
how many deaths
how many folks enslaved in mills
even the grass entrapped, cajoled

civilization's a history of cruelty

see in moor's flung limbs
those deep wounds

ulcers beyond healing

only stone-walling prevents you falling in
keeps from perfection

keeps purpose incomplete

Roger Elkin

The Kiss – Bleaklow

How strange that anything up here
even with frugal ration,
should, in a landscape so severe,
stand as a symbol of voluptuous passion;
of course they're only two big lumps of rock
which look like lips straining towards a kiss,
yet always thwarted of that interlock –
through centuries frustrated of their bliss.
Rodin, when he chose kissing for his theme
gave it a sensual grace –
a swooned succumbing to its lovely dream
that would be out of place
on the harsh desolate moorland here,
with autumn's winds and winter's storms to fear.

Ian M. Emberson

The Peak District: Wolfscote Dale *(Ray Manley)*

The Peak District: Laddow Rocks, Longdendale. The cave at the base of the crag is where rock climbing pioneers used to bivouac *(Bill Bardsley)*

The Peak District: clockwise, from top left – Millstones below Stanage Edge *(Ray Manley)*; Panniers Pool at Three Shire Heads *(Graham Beech)*; Chrome Hill, near Longnor *(Graham Beech)*

The Peak District: early morning spring sunlight in Macclesfield Forest *(Graham Beech)*

Pennine Country

In the beginning
God stuck his thumb-print
on these hills
in peat, sour grass,
the ritual scourging by wind,
and then forgot.

Until the time
our fathers came,
dug-in on slaty scree,
performed their bloody-minded miracle,
conjuring drab towns out of mist,
and still survive in us.

Surely, some day
this doggedness will earn
a blessing,
the peat ooze fat,
the cold streams run wine,
and corn spring from the bare rock.

If not, no matter.
We shall stick it out.
You can't just sling your hook
when the wrong half
belongs to you
by squatter's right.

John Ward

Millstone Grit

From sullen mounds of battered earth
it thrusts its fists at the universe;
millions of years of compressed dust.

A girl there waits, her lover climbs,
his warm breath on the crusted skin.
The spark the rock emits she's seen
in his eyes in the evening light,
and wonders if the rock might too,
within its own great density, have love,

passed on from clay to flesh
as the fragrance of a rose is,
or the wild flower's essence in a wood,
that would speak of love if an essence could.

Wendy Bardsley

Plague Village

Our schools study this place, write projects, or come on coaches
To view its church, the narrow streets, its stocks;
All Summer the cars arrive bringing after-dinner trippers;
They read the plaque and sigh before seeking antiques;
Eyam, plague village.

This Sunday a woman sits reading in a garden of roses
While passing crowds lean across her wall to seek the sign:
'Plague Cottages'. There – behind her – in those mellow houses
Deathly roses once bloomed, ring-a-ringing dying cheeks.
"George Viccars: September 7th. 1665."

Visitors gather round Mompesson's church,
Admire the ancient cross and loiter through the porch,
See his chair, and pause, gathering before an illumined page.
Sydall ... and Derby ... Hancock – Dear God, so many names ....
Eyam, plague village.

We leave for fresher air and stand amongst the flowers.
The trippers seek their coaches, beginning to chatter like sparrows,
Pleased with gifts and cards, pockets full of posies;
But we, being independent, stroll on past stone and roses,
Through a honied afternoon.

As directed, we raise a cover to observe a bull baiting ring,
Then, having eaten too much at Gran's,
Decide on a green climbing path, through purple dead nettle
And wild white parsley, towards Mompesson's well, high above
Eyam, plague village.

An arrow directs us to a stone capped stream, where once goods
And food were left to aid a self-besieged community.
Afterwards I return alone, though with others, through woods
Those few survivors must have trudged.
Dear God, so many names ....

Would I have stayed? George the tailor thought he had a bargain
No doubt, but bought dear at any price, plague cash on delivery.
And those other folk who lived where the old lady reads, they shared
Like good neighbours and died, without choice, here in
Eyam, plague village.

But what of those men of God, William and Thomas? How did they
Persuade to a heroic death folk more used to cheating at cards
Or drinking porter? The waiting must have been worst, examining
Under arms, watching for graves appearing among the neighbour's hay
(Seven in Riley's field.)

Would I have stayed? Could I have stayed,
For the good of others waiting my own death here?
The merest cold, a scent of grass would have sent fear
Sneezing through my brain. Or would I, like the squire, have fled from

Eyam, plague village?

For me the word courage is defined in this narrow place,
In Mompesson and Stanley, in the story of Mistress Hancock
And her seven graves, and in you too gentle Emmott,
With your secret sweetheart and fresh country face.
How could you love

And not flee when Rowland called you to safety,
Across the rocks at Cucklet Delph? There would be no joy
To keep you that Christmas, no carols with the church shut,
No wreathes except on graves, and no one daring to kiss ...
Eyam, plague village.

Of three hundred and fifty villagers, two hundred and fifty nine ...
My modern mind will not focus, seeks comfort amongst the tourists
Until, seeing a plaque not noticed before, I cross to read the dead.
Bagshaw House: six here, and the last one Emmott Sydall. Suddenly
I am crying, standing in a busy street.

Pauline Kirk

Wet Withers

Stone Circle, Eyam Moor, Derbyshire

1

Feebling watermark, three thousand years old
of cleared fields, of graves by a meeting place.

What's our eternity when it's at home:
a page of Shakespeare left out in the rain.

2

Meanwhile, the sky keeps on being a clockface;
the horizon, a calendar, a reckoner
of years: the sun rising from Carl Wark one month
from Higgar Tor the next; the setting moon

shifting further north on Offerton Moor
each winter solstice, then turning south
back to where it started, taking eighteen years
all told, then north again, south again, north again . .

as if the landscape itself was eternal
or the moon was, or come to that, the sun.

John Sewell

The 200th Victim

From the Parish Register of Eyam Church: '1666. August 25th. Katherine Mompesson.'

The village wrapped its poisonous cloak
closely round itself, forcing
the festering sores to ooze within.
A desolate dance with death
performed alone, apart, for love
of those who lived beyond the hills.

Burials were swift; no prayers
no tolling bell; each Sunday
fewer climbed the steep
green slopes of Cucklet Delph
to gather beneath the cragged arch.
Katherine was with them.

Later that August day
walking in sun-soaked fields
She took her husband's hand,
and marvelled at the sweetness of the air;
surely these days of dying must be done?
Somewhere a curlew cried.

Today high on those hills
seven headstones tell
one family's sorrow to the winds,
while in the churchyard
Katherine's tomb
stands near the Saxon Cross.

Peggy Poole

Place of the Plague Wife

for Mrs. Hancocke, who buried a husband and six children when Plague attacked the Derbyshire village of Eyam

Today I stood inside the dry stone ring
which was your land. Despite three hundred years
that separate us, I can hear you sing
your epitaph and taste your salted tears.

Strengthened by constant toil, you must have plied
your husband's fork and spade until release
of tortured limbs replaced the hurt inside.
Alone you watched and nursed, alone you knew
each hope you cherished shrivel as they died.

Did you pray for their souls, or that you too
could learn oblivion? Or standing back
let your unworded wails re-echo through
the rock clefts, paint the morning mountains black?
Did call of cattle force your grieving heart
to common round on empty time's sour track?

Did you have strength enough to make you start
afresh when seven times your love lay deep
interred? Or did pain drag your wits apart?

Colder than stones that mark their graves, you sleep
with them once more. Today a man could pass
this place, not sense the secret woe it keeps.

Today I knotted seven blades of grass –
a ring of roses to protect your rest.

Alison Chisholm

Kinder Trespass

Descending moorland paths through mist,
I peer ahead to spot the marker stone.
A week-day hike, I'm quite alone,
until two boys on mountain bikes appear,

jumping their wheels over earth clods,
bumping and gliding through the clouds.
Across a green-scum bog a wooden bridge
leads to an ancient shooting lodge,

a white hut eerie in the drifting light.
History lives one pace beyond my sight:
country gentlemen, majors, brigadiers,
their entourage of fearsome gamekeepers.

Sixty years ago at William Clough
they confronted Benny Rothman, cyclist,
who dodged police out for his arrest
by peddling all the way from Manchester.

From city slums each young male rambler
took bike or train to open moors,
to cock a snook at trespass laws,
and wade at will each slimy peatland trail.

Hayfield police awaited their return,
dragged Benny and five more to Leicester jail,
incarcerated many months
so gentlemen might shoot wild birds.

The mist thickens, and histories retreat:
through kissing gates I tramp to Hayfield,
where in a small cafe I meet
my bikers guzzling giant mugs of tea.

Brian Cox

Goat

She doesn't mind the isolation
until descending Kinder by the downfall
to Edale she loses the path. It melts
as fog settles. He wouldn't come
doesn't understand how
she can take these peaks so seriously
says he will take her
to the mountains of his childhood.

The mist becomes muscular, fretful
as goats emerge from the grey.
Blurred shivers of animal scuff heels
against the steamy ground.
He once told her that, arriving in Slavkov
late at night, he had clambered
to a tenth floor window
scrambled from balcony to balcony
thought he saw his cousin's light.

Rather than slide uncontrolled
she fumbles for firm earth
glad only goats can see her.
Below is the promiscuous warmth
of the pub, musty embrace of beer
the glancing interest.

A couple escorted him down stairs.
He was drunk, climbed again.
This time the man, watched by the woman
beat him up, called the police.
The cousin was away,
the point had become the scaling of ten floors
a light in a window.

The goats jostle
their stench alien. Rumps knock
against her outstretched arms, lips nip at her face
lick at her sweat. They're too sure-footed.
It's not possible to follow them
now that she needs to get back
to where roads are lit
by the glow of uncurtained sitting rooms.

Jane Kirwan

High Peak

High wind. Always that blast
of cold; raw dawn unleashing
you up the maw of the hill,

your voice ahead like a toddler
racing and falling. Always
too much to remark. But

silence could surprise you:
the inexpressible stalling
somewhere between the gesture

and the word, child-still . .

Below us, cats eyes of
early risers define narrow lanes.
A lantern limps to a field

where a steaming lamb
is slapped by cold. Was it here
we saw that large bird

being driven backward
on the wind? Its huge wings
no more than a weakening protest.

It troubled you then —
With hindsight we read
portents. Now strapped

in your Health Trust chair,
wrapped in a trinity of shawls
you feel the cold, resolutely

watch the play of early light,
how shadows too
effect transformations.

Seán Body

The Legend of Lovers' Leap

They watched, it is said, amazed
As the maid in her crinoline,
Crazed by the jilting, ran
Scorning bramble and thorn
That tried to claw her back,
To the top of the crag where she stood
Her legs coursing with blood.

They watched, it is said, in awe
The fleetness of her rise,
The grimness of her face,
The branding of her glare.
And watched, it is said, in fear
As she stepped onto the air.

One neat little blood-bright foot
And, before the crowd had groaned,
Its pair.

Her crying-out stopped hearts
A hundred miles away,
Three million years ago,
The age before yesterday.
And in the years to be
When a climber in Lycra tights
Would shudder at his stance
As a froth of petticoat frill
Issued from the clouds.

Sharks that ghost the gorge
Marvel at how it was:
How the villagers shut their eyes
To the moment of the smash,
But thinking the falling slow
Again to heaven inclined;
Watched, it is said, amazed
A blackening of the sky,
The gentle downward float
Of a billowing silk-gilled dress,
Two slender blooded legs,
Her forgiving face.

Frances Nagle

Pembrokeshire

From rugged cliffs and islands to secluded tree-lined estuaries and windswept open moorland – these features make up the dramatic landscape of the Pembrokeshire Coast National Park, Britain's only coastal National Park.

It's an ancient landscape steeped in history and legend, underlain by some of the oldest rocks in Britain. People have lived here since early times – and wherever you look you will find their imprint on the landscape. Bronze Age standing stones, Iron Age forts, Norman castles and Victorian fortresses are constant reminders of the past.

Pembrokeshire has a rich and varied culture shaped by the many peoples who have settled here. In the north, the area's Celtic heritage is evident and the Welsh language is strong. The south, which the Normans conquered and settled in the 11th and 12th centuries, is more anglicised. The 'Landsker Line', a chain of Norman fortifications running across the county, still marks the cultural boundary between the two areas.

The coastline and islands are famed for their seabird and seal colonies. Wild flowers flourish in the mild climate, a rich carpet of colour in spring. This stunning coastline can be seen at its best from the spectacular Coast Path, a designated National Trail stretching 186 miles from north to south.

The National Park Authority cares for the area's landscape, wildlife and cultural heritage. It helps to support local communities and promotes opportunities for people to enjoy and understand the area's special qualities.

Rwth Williams, Communications Officer, Pembrokeshire National park

St David's Cathedral

Austerely beautiful it stands
In this green-bastioned glen,
The jewel of the fabled Western land
Beyond the haunts of men;
For here the Norman Leia dreamed and planned,
Building this massive nave,
Pier, arch and architrave,
With skilled, unerring hand,
Of purple stone that knew the shock and roar
Of thundering seas upon the fortressed shore;
And here the Western Wykeham, Gower, wrought
With sure, consummate art,
His chambered rood-screen, where, enmeshed and caught,
In sparkling cusp and crocket here
About his princely bier
And all the visions of a poet's heart.
And like an Oriental dream,
Above the high, triumphant nave is spread
Pole's rich, grey roof of fretted arch and beam,
Each gorgeous carven pendant overhead,
Like damask out of Araby,
While round about the thrusting lantern tower
Burn colour and red heraldry.

Without, stands Gower's palace in array
Of lordly halls and ageless, proud arcades,
Built in the soaring splendour of his prime,
Transfigured by the crafty hands of time
To mellow richness of sublime decay.

So from this place of beauty never fades
The glory of the builders, those who made
With pious, artist hands and hearts aglow
This jewel of the fabled Western land,
In memory, long years ago,
Of one who lived and prayed
In this green-bastioned glen,
St David, Cymric Prince of Christian men.

A.G. Prys-Jones

Tenby

In winter wound in a cocoon of warm
walls, dug discreetly in, snug as a butler
in a pantry, the essential form

of the place remains but all else sleeps;
even the little waves arch neatly on
the sunlit shore with prim and poodle leaps.

Summer romps in on charabanc and train:
sad men in paper caps consume ice-cream
or candy-floss while sheltering from the rain,

and seagulls rest their red, plebeian feet
upon Prince Albert's alabaster head.
But O the joy of Welsh upon the street.

Raymond Garlick

Preseli

Wall of my boyhood, Foel Drigarn, Cam Gyfrwy, Tal Mynydd,
Backing me in all independence of judgment,
And my floor from Y Witwg to Wern and down to Yr Efail
Where the sparks spurted that are older than iron.

And in the yards, on the hearths of my people —
Breed of wind, rain, and mist, of sword-flag and heather,
Wrestling with the earth and the sky and winning
And handing on the sun to their children, from their stooping.

Memory and symbol, a reaping party on their neighbour's
        hillside,
Four swaths of oats falling at every stroke,
And a single swift course, and while stretching their backs
Giant laughter to the clouds, a single peal of four voices.

My Wales, land of brotherhood, my cry, my creed,
Only balm for the world, its message, its challenge,
Pearl of the infinite hour, pledge given by time,
Hope of the long journey on the short winding way.

This was my window, the harvesting and the shearing.
I beheld order in my palace there.
A roar, a ravening, is roaming the windowless forest.
Let us guard the wall from the beast, keep the well-spring free
        of the filth.

Waldo Williams

Translated by Joseph P. Clancy

Coal Seams at Newgale

The sun is a cold disc
Above the sea-mist;
Our voices echo
Like luminous thin cries
Inside a box of light.

'Come on, dad, take us to the caves
Until it clears.'

And so we walk a causeway
Shining between mist, until the cliffs
Lean over us and stare in a cold sweat.

We scramble on pebbles, shout in the cracks,
Squeeze between pillars of rock
Until, caught off balance,
I rest my hand
Against the soft wetness of coal.
Unmistakable.
Like scrapings from slurry-screens
Where cascades of water once soaked
My dad's vest.

A boy again, smiling with fear,
I watch his shovel glint,
Hear the rasp of his lungs
As he works at the clogging mess of coal,
Always losing the race, always
Wanting his shift to end.

Until it did.

'Dad, dad, the sun's out.'

In the brightness
I stare at the sea
Where the coal seams are running unseen
Out of Wales, out of time,
Not to break surface again
Where my hand might rest on his.

Mike Sharpe

Seal Island

(Caldey Island, Pembrokeshire)

seal curved sleeping island
grey skinned under channel wind

from your glistening back trees
bracken giant ferns rise

above the red and white monastery
nestling in deep skin-folds

surrounded by gulls you bask
eyes shut, frozen to stone

yet we half expect you to slide
oil-smooth over rocks vanishing
under green atlantic waves

Alison J. Bielski

The Lighthouse at Strumble Head

In the clean house on the rock
where sleepy headlands drink the evening sea
and floors are cut to fit horizons,
the great fish-eye revolves
in a socket that floats on mercury.

Waters slide and close over the drowned,
their bones add salt to salt, grains
among the sand, cries in the gull's throat.
Ninety years the beam has loomed
the century's night.

In early times it took a man's sleeve
bursting to flame one placid afternoon
as he dipped his arm between the stilled facets,
to learn that, if revolution ceased at sunrise,
daylight could turn its eye in on itself

and burn the heart like a collapsing star,
as a child learns fire by capturing the sun
in a magnifying glass
to make Excalibur.

Gillian Clarke

Annie *(1868-1944)*

I called her Ga, and a child's stuttered
syllable became her name.
A widow nearly forty years,
beautiful and straight-backed,
always with a bit of lace about her,
pearls the colour of her twisted hair,
the scent of lavender.

It was our job at Fforest to feed the hens
with cool and liquid handfuls of thrown corn.
We looked for eggs smuggled in hedge and hay,
and walked together the narrow path to the sea
calling the seals by their secret names.

At Christmas she rustled packages under her bed
where the po was kept and dusty suitcases.
That year I got an old doll with a china face,
ink-dark eyes and joints at elbows and knees.
Inside her skull, like a tea-pot, under her hair,
beneath her fontanelle, was the cold cave
where her eye-wires rocked her to sleep.

Somewhere in a high hospital window –
I drive past it sometimes with a start of loss –
her pale face made an oval in the glass
over a blue dressing-gown. She waved to me,
too far away to be certain it was her.
They wouldn't let children in.
Then she was lost or somebody gave her away.

*

First spring day in the hills.
Hens laid wild in stack and hedge.
In my palm the ice-egg
was stupidly heavy and still.

Crude pot-egg, overblown acorn
colour of bone, of fungi,
of old stone bottles,
a stone to crack a jaw.

Not delicate
like Nain's china eggs,
crazed little stone skulls,
false pregnancy, fool's gold.

Easily fooled the old hen
panicked to quicken it
under her breast-down. Stone
under the heart, stillborn.

Gillian Clarke

Dylan Thomas at Tenby

Into the pause, while peppermints were passed
after the strong piano's breathless Brahms,
he walked and took his place, sat down and cast

(expressionless of face) an eye abroad,
moving the carafe with a marked distaste.
His fame proclaimed, he looked politely bored

and crossed his legs and lit a cigarette,
screwing his eyes up at the smart of smoke.
So all was done and said. The scene was set

for speech, and nervously he stirred and spoke —
shuffling the pack of papers on his knee,
at random drew one, stared at it and woke

into awareness. Now the sleeping town
under the wood of Wales sat up and sang,
rose from its river bed and eiderdown

of ducks, strode heron-stilted through the dark
and rode white horses, nightmares from the sea,
across a cantref to this bay's bright arc

and the Noah of a poet calling there
to his creatures to come. Two by two, word
by word they marched from his mouth, pair by pair

to the beat of the drum of his tongue
and the trumpet of his lips. In the ships
of his speech the sage sailed and was sung.

And Tenby, their harbour, attended.
It was October, the month of birthdays.
The saga was nearly ended.

Raymond Garlick

Pembrokeshire: Monkstone
beach & Waterwynch bay on
the south Pembrokeshire
coastline. Between
Saundersfoot & Tenby,
several secluded sandy
beaches are revealed at low
tide *(Pembrokeshire County
Council)*

Pembrokeshire: above — The Preseli Hills, famous for the bluestones which were transported to Stonehenge on Salisbury Plain 2,000 years ago; left — Tenby North Beach, viewed from the harbour end. Goscar Rock is in the foreground *(Pembrokeshire County Council)*

Approaching Little Haven on the Pembrokeshire coastal path *(Sheila Lewis)*

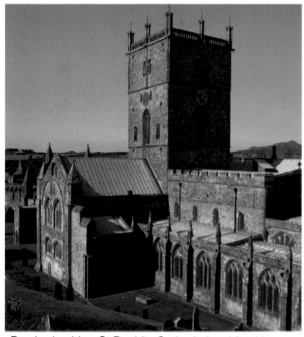

Pembrokeshire: St David's Cathedral, spiritual home
of Wales *(Pembrokeshire County Council)*

The ruined church of Cwm-yr-Eglwys on the
Pembrokeshire coastal path *(Sheila Lewis)*

Snowdonia

The glaciers of the last Ice Age moulded the dramatic Snowdonia landscape of deep valleys and rugged mountains. Rivers, lakes and waterfalls, and remnants of ancient deciduous woodland, are typical of the Park; as is the coast along the shores of Cardigan Bay, with its sandy bays and dunes, and the three beautiful estuaries – Glaslyn/Dwyryd, Mawddach and Dyfi.

A rich variety of plants and wildlife, which includes the unique Snowdon Lily and the Gwyniad in the depths of LIyn Tegid, mirrors the diversity of the landscape, and the whole of Snowdonia is a stronghold of the Welsh language and way of life.

Archaeological remains from the Neolithic period, the Bronze and Iron Ages, the Roman occupation and the Middle Ages survive, as does evidence of the recent industrial past of gold, lead and copper mining, and slate quarrying on a grand scale.

Barbara Jones, Information Officer, Snowdonia National Park Authority

Cader Idris

I
The mountain was warmer then
as I shinned its green slopes
to the polished peak,
to where God had sat on the seventh day
to bless the Mawddach estuary.

In the towering sêt-fawr
I recited the names of Quaker farms
quivering below in the hot fields
from Gelli-lwyd to Bryncrug.

And with the sun,
a red coracle on the sea,
down to ty Nain for cold meat and pickle,
scuttling into bed from the ghosts
groaning in the tall dark wardrobes.

II
Today,
my head heavy with the night's beer,
the slopes were steeper,
the rocks sharper.

Above Llyn Cau
clouds heaved with rain,
and those with faith
strong enough to move mountains
crawled like ladybirds on the distant ridge.

Below, twisting in the mist,
the path to the warm cwm.

Huw Jones

A Mountain Rescue

Safe, from the farmhouse window
we watched in the gathering dusk
the helicopter, jewelled with navigation lights
more splendidly than any gaudy insect,
circle the black cone of Tryfan,
endlessly manoeuvring to gain or lose
a few feet of height, some balance of thrusts.

It was curiously beautiful, yet the beauty
we could not have seen but for the terrible fall
of a climber missing his handhold in
the blustering wind.

Having been glad to see the aerial
dance of the machine, so much more beautiful
by dusk than by day, we were glad
to hear of the rescue and to know
that this strange and jewelled machine
carried a precise and practical compassion,
as, safe, from the farmhouse window
we watched in the gathering dusk
its gaudy insect rite that rendered mercy.

Frederic Vanson

Eidyllion

The crags of Snowdon cry
in creaking wind —
does Arthur sleep within?
   Bones of sheep
   whiten the cwms.

The rocks of Tryfan sigh
in shrouding snow —
does Bedivere lie here?
   Ravens rise
   at Dinas Emrys.

And the waters of Llyn Llydaw
whisper to the shore —
does Excalibur rest below?
   Samite fish
   hide in the rushes.

Gladys Mary Coles

From: *The Prelude*

Book Thirteen

In one of these excursions, travelling then
Through Wales on foot, and with a youthful Friend,
I left Bethgelert's huts at couching-time,
And westward took my way to see the sun
Rise from the top of Snowdon. Having reached
The Cottage at the Mountain's foot, we there
Rouz'd up the Shepherd, who by ancient right
Of office is the Stranger's usual guide;
And after short refreshment sallied forth.

It was a Summer's night, a close warm night,
Wan, dull and glaring, with a dripping mist
Low-hung and thick that cover'd all the sky,
Half threatening storm and rain; but on we went
Uncheck'd, being full of heart and having faith
In our tried Pilot. Little could we see
Hemm'd round on every side with fog and damp,
And, after ordinary traveller's chat
With our Conductor, silently we sank
Each into commerce with his private thoughts:
Thus did we breast the ascent, and by myself
Was nothing either seen or heard the while
Which took me from my musings, save that once
The Shepherd's Cur did to his own great joy
Unearth a hedgehog in the mountain crags
Round which he made a barking turbulent.
This small adventure, for even such it seemed
In that wild place and at the dead of night,
Being over and forgotten, on we wound
In silence as before. With forehead bent
Earthward, as if in opposition set
Against an enemy, I panted up
With eager pace, and no less eager thoughts.
Thus might we wear perhaps an hour away,
Ascending at loose distance each from each,
And I, as chanced, the foremost of the Band:
When at my feet the ground appear'd to brighten,
And with a step or two seem'd brighter still;
Nor had I time to ask the cause of this,
For instantly a Light upon the turf
Fell like a flash: I looked about, and lo!
The Moon stood naked in the Heavens, at height
Immense above my head, and on the shore
I found myself of a huge sea of mist,
Which, meek and silent, rested at my feet:
A hundred hills their dusky backs upheaved
All over this still Ocean, and beyond,

Far, far beyond, the vapours shot themselves,
In headlands, tongues, and promontory shapes,
Into the Sea, the real Sea, that seem'd
To dwindle, and give up its majesty,
Usurp'd upon as far as sight could reach.
Meanwhile, the Moon look'd down upon this shew
In single glory, and we stood, the mist
Touching our very feet; and from the shore
At distance not the third part of a mile
Was a blue chasm; a fracture in the vapour,
A deep and gloomy breathing-place through which
Mounted the roar of waters, torrents, streams
Innumerable, roaring with one voice.
The universal spectacle throughout
Was shaped for admiration and delight,
Grand in itself alone, but in that breach
Through which the homeless voice of waters rose,
That dark deep thoroughfare had Nature lodg'd
The Soul, the Imagination of the whole.

William Wordsworth

Snowdonia

Black on white, a roadside, a shock
of mountain rock: I am looking in
through a photo found in an Indian tin,
to a piece of forgotten history.
There on my father's knee,
my hair cut like Clara Bow,
I can't have been more than three.

Do I remember, or is it a dream
that the group of relations, resting
on stones, are exhausted to mutiny,
while my father continues to
urge us upward? My eyes
look shyly under my fringe
at whatever he wants me to see.

For a moment I imagine his voice:
'The air, taste the air.' And my throat
tightens, searching the square
of a black and white photo,
a band of ghosts, and a
mountain's majestic glare.

Elaine Feinstein

Rhaiadr Du

'Black Waterfall', Dolgellau, Snowdonia

As if courting it –
each day for three days
walking there through frosted woods.

We'd lean, weight forward
where it lunges over –
three spreading tails of water

the spray-mist glazed
on rocks, a jutting branch
englassed, each turf spike

a clear feather of ice.
Only its sound
between us.

Everything was waterfall,
no matter how furious
or slow, movement

was immaterial.
A minute went by,
then another.

From where we stood
the sky had new light –
intelligible fire.

John Sewell

Snowdonian

(From: *Mountains*, Part 1)

'O the mind, mind has mountains ...' (Hopkins)

At the start of our climbing career
Each had his flask, his blue cagoule
And a uniform will to be first
In the sprint to the peak;
Nobody thought it was steep
Or fell far out of step.

So, back at the gabled hostel,
There were coffee and biscuits, a perfect
Unnecessary roll-call,
Viollet, Wavering,
White, Wood,
And no weak link exposed;

Though on the downward scree
Slipping and dying in jest
Twyford (2Y) had spotted a single
Classic sure-foot, bearded goat
Lost to the herd, broken-backed
Among heathery boulders.

Mick Imlah

Lightning Rod

On storm-cloud days he'd meander mountain ridges
inhale the summits of Tryfan or Crib Goch
upstretch his cane threaded with mercury
exhort its tip to blossom in St Elmo's Fire
inciting lightning to strike it
skelter the silver, link of copper wire,
plunge into the flask strapped to his belt.

He'd no illusions about lightning's power
to turn desert sand into glass serpents,
water into wine, innocents to prophets;
it ignited Moses' beard on Ararat,
quickened our barren earth
by ripping primal molecules apart

- ripped Wilco, fifty years ago. On the ridge,
unmarked, until a fumbled unbuttoning
- a scarlet fern stamped on his chest.

To tame it he must understand, so every night
by oil-light in his garden shed
he galvanised gold-leaf and pith, made sparks
by rubbing rabbit fur on ebonite or amber,
loaded Leyden jars with electric energy,
turned the handle on his Wimshurst machine
- and as it spat and crackled
the smell of soil and carrots deepened.

His vision, to come down from the mountain
with a flask of violet water, boiling quietly,
feeding on the lightning trapped inside
bleeding away: emasculated

as Wilco who once could back-flip fences,
hop the playground on one hand, wouldn't cry
no matter how hard Shelley thrashed him: Wilco

who'd convinced him he could shed his callipers,
whose flesh he'd touched just once
- hairless chest, cold, burning.

Campers in the cwm said flickering light
had shown him, arm extended, in staccato dance
until a flash still stamped onto their eyeballs
froze him, on Tryfan,
balanced on one hand, in glory.

Lilac scent of ozone, gold tooth welded to his specs.

John Latham

Snowdonia: Crib Goch (foreground) and Crib y Ddysgl, leading to the summit of Snowdon *(Graham Beech)*

Snowdonia: sunset over Llyn Ogwen *(Ikon Imaging)*

Snowdonia: Castell y Gwynt — the Castle of The Winds — is one of the many incredible landscape features to be found on the Glyder range above the Ogwen Valley *(Graham Beech)*

Cottage in Snowdonia

'Each worker of no less than ten years standing
shall be granted seven eighths part of an acre
and the right to a dwelling for his habitation
provided it be constructed within a single day,
smoke rising from its chimney before midnight.'

And so, one Sunday, in 1748, sleepy lanterns
straggled up the hill: they worked all day
with pick and adze on granite, slate and oak,
one small break for cheese and ale. No time
for scaffolding, so walls could not be higher
than Dai, the biggest lad, could lift a rock.

In 1998, a man looks out from an old window
on a view they would have seen: Moel Eilio,
Caernarfon, Menai Straits, a fishing-boat,
a shadow in the sky that might be Ireland.
He rests his forehead on a yard-thick wall,
asks what it retains from that first day.

Images seep in: a farthing Gwynneth placed
for luck under the hearth-stone; buttermilk
that dripped from Owen's beard; salt-grains
from sweat that rolled from naked shoulders;
smear of blood when Megan scraped her thigh.

The shapes of fingertips in long-dried mud
when Llewelyn's hand closed over Sian's,
and in one sweet, bitter second they tried
to live the lifetime they would have shared
if she were not already pledged to Griff.

John Latham

Tryfan

Surely some stormgathering god remains here!
Shrouded in steamy cloud the mountain frowns
Over the leaden lake, a god of anger,
A raingiver, drenching at times the floodplain,
Swelling at times the tithing streams that roar his fear
Where thunderous waters fall from the lake's end.

Rising steep as a wall his fastness dwarfs
The hardwon works of man. Unbeautiful
In a land of beautiful mountains, this giant, black,
Barren, bleak, cloudgathering point

Broods over the small water meadows, frowns
On the windlashed, cold llyn,
And, sinister even in summer, holds court
With the manysided winds.

Surely some hammerwielding god, older than man,
Remains here, rockbound but reverberating
In sudden thunder, prisoner of his own
Eight-winded kingdom, till darkness shall fall again
And the green hopes of man are finally humbled,
And the death of the sapraising sun
Leaves him his sway, unchallenged and eternal.

Frederic Vanson

The Yorkshire Dales

What a place I have found, of white crags and shining stones, where heather embroiders high hills and meadow-flowers carpet valley floors, where waterfalls crash and secret caverns lie underfoot. What a place I have found where landscapes collide, a place called the Yorkshire Dales.

Early in the year, in the dawn light rising over the valley of Swaledale, the sheep graze on tough heather, the water-logged ground is treacherous with hidden ice, and a freezing wind whips the cheeks and fills the ears of those who venture over the bleak high paths.

Later, when the summer sun has warmed the land, the children on Wharfedale enjoy a sublime playground of sun-baked grass and paddle their hot feet in the cooling currents of the river. From a nearby farm comes the buzz of machinery and the sweet scent of the mown hay.

And at the close of the year, the setting sun casts shadows over secret places where ancient kings rested on long journeys, sheltered in the valley of Kingsdale. Where golden sunlight reflects on gilded heathland, and slabs of dark stone form thrones where wanderers may sit and rest.

The Yorkshire Dales, a landscape formed by the interaction of human labour and nature, a special place because of what *you* might find.

Cassandra Tebb, *Communications Officer, Yorkshire Dales National Park Authority*

Pennines in April

If this country were a sea (that is solid rock
Deeper than any sea) these hills heaving
Out of the east, mass behind mass, at this height
Hoisting heather and stones to the sky
Must burst upwards and topple into Lancashire.

Perhaps, as the earth turns, such ground-stresses
Do come rolling westward through the locked land.
Now, measuring the miles of silence
Your eye takes the strain: through

Landscapes gliding blue as water
Those barrellings of strength are heaving slowly and heave
To your feet and surf upwards
In a still, fiery air, hauling the imagination,
Carrying the larks upward.

Ted Hughes

A Yorkshire Mask-Maker

for Ken Smith

Under a yellow lamp
under a yellow shiver of light

see how a sharp stab of the thumbs
makes the clay stare.

And even though this is a city
and the air is thick with coughing
and smells of barbecues and curry,

in that brow we can trace
the arched wings of an owl

as it swoops from the Pennines
to its prey.

Then lower, the mask-maker's hands
smooth the chin
to match the curve of his heart.

All tomorrow, from the clay mouth
we'll hear
the white owl calling.

Danielle Hope

In Swaledale

In Swaledale lal Tommy Woof sits up,
A lone cow calving in the byre's his charge.
She nuzzles the stall and Tommy fills his cup
From the flask. Above the Corpse Way and the yard

A hard moon rubs the margin of the dale,
Troubled by coming clouds.
A yowe stands, graven by the river's edge
A bat, a sudden slash in the air sails out

Orbits the barn once and is gone. From a ledge
As a light rain starts to fall, hunting owls call.

In Dentdale lovers lie below a bridge
Entangled legs and soft cries and soft calls,
A tawny owl slides overhead sweet as a moth
Sees the pale flesh hears the murmurs fall.

In Ribblesdale a signal-man talks down
The line to Settle, horse names, odds, times,
And the television news, family, friends;
Celebrating the ways of men to men.

And over all of this, Lal Tommy's house,
The signal box, the lovers in the barn
Softer than the dust from any moth's wing,
Softer than the skin of any calf.

Softer than any lover's wet-mouthed after-kiss
The soft rain from Chernobyl falls.

Mike Harding

A Burial at Horton

The last of our adopted fathers, now—
on this green-island day, amid wild snows—
after an absence has come back for good
to lay his big, slow-moving farmer's bones
in Horton churchyard where schoolfellows lie
under the disappearing local names:
    Bill Redmayne, Mason Baines, Beck Heseltine.

You started up at Dub Cote, with one horse,
then marvelled that you owned the Squire's old house
and worked a double farm. Hard work did well,
but you're set in the past now, with the Squire,
and lines of men with rakes to turn green swathes
to hay, and Mary Ellen bringing tea,
    and all the fragrant grass of eighty years.

When we first came, your son was newly wed;
then, hand in hand, over the emerald ground,
he and his bride walked out to tend the lambs.
Now my first son, then crying like a lamb,
is grown through more than twenty lambing-times
and gone away, leaving his ghost behind
    with this year's children fishing in the beck.

The snowdrifts underline the drystone walls.
Olympian plaster mountains stare, aloof,
over green drumlin hills where you're at home:
where "more snow comes to fetch old drifts away"
and "it's two topcoats colder on the fells"
and "never right warm when yon mountain's white,"
    and you were born, and knew thy way about.

You gave their first pay-packets to my boys
one haytime, and you said they worked like men.
Were they about sixteen? They came home late
on Summer nights bright with the haytime moon,
blind-drunk on work, and milk dipped from the churn,
and supper on the newly-shaven ground,
    smelling of sweat and hayseeds, oil, machines.

Those lads are in the past now, with the men
of the old village, who were lads with you
in this green hammock slung from those white peaks,
and children playing games along "the Flat"
before the lorries commandeered all roads
such as the winding, one-way, switchback track
    that brought us here and will not take us back.

Your Sabbath-keeping used to rest the horse,
but tractors broke the custom. Breaking down,

machines keep random sabbaths of their own.
You mastered barns full of the new machines
but change from hay to silage finished you,
moving your landmarks round while you stood by.
     A full-time Sabbath claimed you in the end.

Stealing your cautious smile and careful thought
out of our sight and into history,
the plodding pace of one who walks all day
and never hurries, brought you to this place
where you are folded in, under the turf
spread with snow-fleeces, like a shearing ground,
     beside your wife, among the village names.

Bill Redmayne: Mason Baines: Beck Heseltine:
Jack Lambert, John, Meg in her haytime hat:
John Dinsdale, Dinsdale daughters, let Bob in.
The village of his boyhood swings its gate.
The grave heals first with snow, and then with grass:
then with forgetfulness. New villagers
     we shuffle up towards the empty place.

                              Anna Adams

A Man Must Climb

A man must climb his mountain-side of years
And from each conquered height of age or fame
Look down above the precipice of fears,
The bogs of doubt, and see the way he came;
How every venturous mile was rich with gifts,
Streams where he thirsted, scented turf for rest,
And so press on into the mountain rifts
No wanderer, but a long-expected guest,
Until he feels full in his face and free
The summit-wind of high eternity.

                              Showell Styles

Mill Stones

You have to seek there now for human sounds
above the track up from Gunnar's meadow
like ore among the desolate spoil-heaps:
piles of soiled skulls beneath
the wind keening over fell-tops
the colour of pewter
bruised with heather,
and spiked with young bracken
that's returning to ground made bald
and sickened from the flues. Above
the liquid bleating of curlew
and lapwing wail across a moonscape
made by men, blank pastures
of decay where women and their children
kibbled at the Old Gang mines.

The smelting mills are rubbled now
by Hard Level Gill, but for a high
square chimney, a cenotaph intact.
There by the chemistry of fire and sweat
lead was once made gold for other men
far beyond the dale.

Men have bored here for centuries
treated like maggots mostly —
convict Brigantes chained in
by Romans, and more recently
miners with lead in their veins,
grey and early in their graves.

From the chimney and furnace walls
I've extracted some chunks of stone
still glazed under a dry scab of ore:
seemingly reddened in the smelting
to the colour of blood,
rusted by widows' pains.

Rodney Pybus

Yorkshire Dales: above Aysgarth Falls *(Graham Beech)*

Yorkshire Dales: Swaledale
(Ikon Imaging)

Yorkshire Dales: limestone pavement *(Yorkshire Dales National Park)*

Foxes

Foxes are canine cats, feline terriers,
scavengers of country garbage,
who'll blitz the charnel hen-coop
to lay up next month's carrion supper.

But foxes can be kept by man and humbled.
They will adjust to the human, grades
of familiarity marking descent
from the wild.
They'll snap at biscuits and cheese
and tumble like yapping cat-dogs
down the slope with man.

Tense nerves they keep, and that rancid
foxy stench like Camembert gone mad —
but they lose that tensile self-preserving fear
of man.

Lean tan Yorkshire jackal,
predator of alfresco lunches for whose crumbs
the dog-fox must wait, the vixen
yawns and dozes at the limits
of twenty feet of domestic chain —
almost like a puppy
till she looks you in the eye:

then the cat comes out
with a pale and wary glare
of pitiless topaz, backlit
with memories of the kill.

Rodney Pybus

High Intake Dale

Over bleak tops: neglected walls,
slant thorns (if any trees at all)
and tousled sheep tell of long wars
to wrest a living from such hills.

A sign says S or Z, the lane
dips down and zigzags to a dale
whose fields incline towards a tarn—
dead-level in its hill-rimmed bowl.

About the lake, some scattered farms:
High Intake, Whitber, Mosscrop and
Cold Cotes and Newlands. Drystone walls
hold grazing sheep and meadow land,

and bright-leaved little woods, as green
as May, and maytrees white as snow
with still-untarnished blossom, though
high Summer in the vale below

darkened the leaves and overgrew
wild roadside gardens. There the hay
was cut and dried, raked up and baled,
borne to the barn and stored away

already, but up here the hum
of tractors told of haytime still
in progress. Time had been reversed
to June as we had climbed uphill.

We couldn't find it on the map
so asked a woman by a gate
the valley's name: she said 'It's called
the Dale where Spring comes late.'

She smiled at us, triumphantly;
not young, she wore some beauty yet:
'But I would never move elsewhere,'
she said, 'for I am used to it.

'I was born here: the farm is mine,
my daughter turns the swathes down there
beside the lake; my husband mows
High Meadow; forecasts promise fair.'

'It's such a lovely place,' we said;
'so green and fresh. It was too warm
down in the valley bottom.' 'Days
like this,' she says, 'do us no harm.

'But you should see the frozen lake:
a floor of ice, felted with snow,
roofing the long-drowned church, crisscrossed
by tracks where neighbours come and go

from Intake Farm to Newlands Farm,
Cold Cotes to Whitber or Mosscrop,
while snow blocks up the road you took
today, from walltop to walltop.

'Less than six weeks ago, it snowed;
Midsummer's day, the tops were white.
I've learned to bear the climate's rude
practical jokes and catspaw spite.

'Bright flowers nod beside my house;
I keep an ancient apple tree.
No one could say it bears much fruit
but it seems sweet to me.

Anna Adams

Thermodynamics

I saw beyond the blackboard and the bare wall,
Beyond the abstract, confining symbols
A rough and simple cliff, ascending in steep tiers
To fade in mist-bound mystery.

I travelled time and space to feel again
The grip of Vibram soles on weathered rock,
The trustful uplift of the body
On holds made safe by balance
Held in fingertip subjection;
I heard rope-rustle on the shelving slabs,
Friends' laughter and the headstrong wind;
I smelt the dew-damp heather, and
The gentle scent of turf and moss;
I saw the elemental rock,
Flecked with colour, scarped and wrinkled,
Cheerfully give way to skill;
Sudden sunshine on the crags,
And other ranges, distance-blue,
Guarding shadowed valleys;
I tasted joy, more wholesome sweet
Than pleasure and not cloying.
I knew the freedom of fellowship
Knit with stronger bonds than nylon.

I offered humble thanks, and quietly
Came back to the Lecture Room.

Martyn Berry

On Dodd Fell

for Ray Fisher

People seem meaningless
among so much abstract nature, the weather
that decides a shade of green, or shades
in forested hillside that falls to the valley like water
and among the huge wide moor.
Blobs of colour translate to gortex,
a tiny car running defines a road.
I know that road meets a smaller
that leads, winding out the gradient,
                    to a little town
and people, a meal, a joke invented
            over a pint, about Beethoven
so deaf he thought he was a painter.

Wensleydale, a friendly name,
its green-wax wheel of cheese local
but prized everywhere. Up here
it's a farmed wilderness that cuts art
            down to size,
the wind deafening and the gusts of rain
                        easing off
to a late sonata of a landscape
saying nothing much through this anomaly,
me, compared even to a copy
from a wide-angled lens:
easier to take in and eloquent
beyond words, like music.

Peter Sansom

Acknowledgements

Grateful thanks must go to the publishers below for permission to reprint copyright material. I would also like to thank Manchester Metropolitan University Library, John Rylands University Library, Manchester, London Central Reference Library, David Bromwich, Somerset Studies Library, Taunton, David Barren, Lancaster University Library, Sandra Matthews, The County Library, Pembrokeshire, Aylsham Library, Norfolk, and in particular, Bernard Watkins and David Brinn, Brecon Beacons National Park Authority, Jill Renney, North York Moors National Park Authority, Brian Pearce, Exmoor National Park Authority and John Weir, Dartmoor National Park Authority for their valuable assistance. Lastly, I must extend my appreciation to Tom Waghorn for his interest and support and Graham Beech for giving me this splendid project.

Jazz Festival, ROLAND MATHIAS, A Field at Vallorcines, (Gomer Press, 1996). My Son on Castell Dinas, CHRISTOPHER MEREDITH, (Poetry Wales, Vol. 32, July, 1995). Quarry, ANNE CLUYSENAAR, Timeslips, (Carcanet, 1997). On Pen Y Fan, BRIAN MORRIS, (Gomer Press, 1967). The Lady of Llyn Y Fan Fach, NIGEL JENKINS, Ambush, (Gomer Press, 1998).

Norfolk, JOHN BETJEMAN, Collected Poems, compiled by Lord Birkenhead, (John Murray, 1988). East Anglian Bathe, JOHN BETJEMAN, Ibid. The Field, Tomorrow, GEORGE MAGBETH, Poems from Oby, Seeker & Warburg, 1982. Barton Broad, MARY GARDNER, From Songs of The Broads, (The Asphodel Press.) The Deserted Aerodrome, MABEL FERRETT, Scathed Earth, (University of Saltzburg, 1996).

New Year on Dartmoor, SYLVIA PLATH, Collected Poems, (Faber & Faber, 1981.) Usurpur Stone, JOHN POWLS, Dartmoor Dreams (Devon Books, 1995). Small Talk at Wreyland, PATRICIA BEER, Autumn, (Carcanet Press Ltd., 1998). Princetown, U.A. FANTHORPE, Standing To, (Peterloo Poets, 1982). Standing on the Brink of Light, WILLIAM OXLEY, In The Drift Of Words, (Rockingham Press, 1992).

Kabla Khun, DOUGLAS DUNN, Dante's Drum Kit, (Faber & Faber, 1993). Bagley Combe, DINAH LIVINGSTONE, May Day, (Katabasis, London, 1997).

Wordsworth's Umbrella, GLADYS MARY COLES, New & Selected Poems, (Duckworth, 1986). From a Boat at Coniston, NORMAN NICHOLSON, Selected Poems, (Faber & Faber, 1982). Spring Images Above Coniston, JOHN WARD, A Late Harvest, (Peterloo Poets, 1982). The Walk, WILLIAM SCAMMELL, Five Easy Pieces, (Sinclair-Stevenson, 1993). Skiddaw House, DAVID SCOTT, Selected Poems, (Bloodaxe Books, 1998). Going out from Ambleside, FLEUR ADCOCK, Selected Poems, (Oxford University Press, 1983).

Walltown Crags, JOHN WARD, A Late Harvest, (Peterloo Poets, 1982). Northumberland, JOHN WARD, (Never Bury Poetry, 1998). Recent History, GERARD WOODWARD, Island to Island, (Chatto & Windus, 1999). Routing Linnby, RODNEY PYBUS, Bridging Loans, (Chatto & Windus,

1976). The Journey, KATHLEEN RAINE, Collected Poems, (George Allen & Unwin Ltd., 1981). Poem found at Chesters Museum, Hadrian's Wall, FRANCES HOROVITZ, Collected Poems, (Bloodaxe Books, 1985). The Roman Wall, ANDREW YOUNG, Selected Poems, (Carcanet, 1998). Cheviot Autumn, JOHN WARD, A Late Harvest, (Peterloo Poets, 1982).

Gorse, and Between The Heather and the Sea, PETER MORGAN, A Winter Visitor, (Secker & Warburg, 1983). Roots in Lastingham, JOHN WARD, Grandfather Best & The Protestant Work Ethic, (Littlewood, 1991).

Pennine Country, JOHN WARD, A Late Harvest, (Peterloo Poets, 1982). Plague Village, PAULINE KIRK, Red Marl and Brick, (Littlewood, 1985). The 200th Victim, PEGGY POOLE, No Wilderness in Them, (Merseyside Mini Booklets, 1984).

St. David's Cathedral, A.G. PRYS-JONES, Collected Poems of A.G. Prys-Jones, edited by Don Dale-Jones, (Gomer Press, 1988). Tenby, RAYMOND GARLICK, Collected Poems, (Gomer Press, 1987). Preseli, WALDO WILLIAMS (Translated by Joseph P. Clancy) The Peacemakers, edited by Tony Conran, (Gomer Press, 1997). Coal Seams at Newgale, MIKE SHARPE, Thoughts Like an Ocean, Pont Books, (Gomer Press, 1997) Seal Island, (Caldey Island, Pembrokeshire) ALISON J. BIELSKI, ibid. Annie 1868-1944 + The Lighthouse, GILLIAN CLARKE, Collected Poems, (Carcanet Press Ltd., 1997) Dylan Thomas at Tenby, RAYMOND GARLICK, Collected Poems, (Gomer Press, 1987).

Cader Idris, HUW JONES, A Small Field, (Gomer Press, 1985). A Mountain Rescue, FREDERIC VANSON, Spring at Lyn Ogwen, (Gomer Press, 1972). Eidyllon, GLADYS MARY COLES, Leafburners, New & Selected Poems, (Duckworth, 1986). Rhaiadr Du, JOHN SEWELL, Bursting The Clouds, (Jonathan Cape, 1998) Snowdonian, MICK IMLAH, Birthmarks, (Chatto & Windus, 1994). Tryfan, FREDERIC VANSON, Spring at Lyn Ogwen, (Gomer Press, 1972).

Pennines in April, TED HUGHES, Lupercal, (Faber & Faber, 1960). In Swaledale, MIKE HARDING, Daddy Edgar's Pools, (Peterloo Poets, 1992). A Burial at Horton, ANNA ADAMS, Trees in Sheep Country, (Peterloo Poets, 1986). Mill Stones, RODNEY PYBUS, In Memoriam Milena, (Chatto & Windus, 1973). Foxes, RODNEY PYBUS, ibid. A Yorkshire Mask-Maker, DANIELLE HOPE, City Fox, (Rockingham Press, 1998). High Intake Dale, ANNA ADAMS, Nobodies, (Peterloo Poets, 1990).

Also of Interest

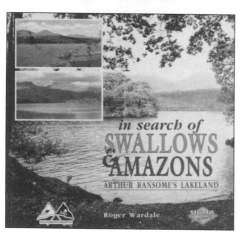

THE CONISTON TIGERS: 70 Years of Mountain Adventure
A. Harry Griffin

This is the life story of A. Harry Griffin MBE, much loved as Country Diary writer for *The Guardian*. Of interest to lovers of the great outdoors, and to those who simply enjoy writing of the highest calibre, "The Coniston Tigers" features period photographs of climbers from the 1930s with their minimal climbing gear — some nonchalantly smoking their pipes as they balance on the most delicate ledge. "A very special book . . . a living history of modern Lakeland climbing" — Chris Bonington. "The book which thousands have been willing Harry Griffin to write." — Alan Rusbridger, Editor of *The Guardian*. "Prose tumbles off the page as clear as a mountain stream." — Bill Birkett, mountain writer & photographer."... one of the great outdoor writers of the century." — Cameron McNeish, Editor of *The Great Outdoors*. *£9.95*

IN SEARCH OF SWALLOWS & AMAZONS: Arthur Ransome's Lakeland
Roger Wardale

This is a new edition of a popular book published in 1986. Additional material has been added to satisfy even the most avid reader of "Swallows & Amazons" — three decades of Ransome hunting with text and photographs to identify the locations of the ever-popular series of books. There's a two-fold pleasure in this book — enjoying the original stories and discovering the farms, rivers, islands, towns and hills that formed their backdrop. *£7.95*

THE DRAGON'S TRAIL: Wales on Horseback
Paula Brackston

Two women, two horses, and over two hundred miles of breathtaking Welsh countryside... This day-by-day journal is a record of the fresh perspective travelling by horseback gave of Wales — a magical country of contrasts and change. Her lively, lyrical, often humorous account not only tells of her experiences of the Welsh landscape, but the views and anecdotes of the people she encountered on the way. Includes a route map, ideas on how to plan a similar or shorter ride, plus information on little-known parts of Wales. *£5.95*

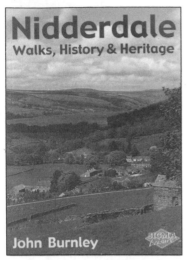

NIDDERDALE: Walks, History & Heritage
John Burnley

Nidderdale is the smallest of the Yorkshire Dales, between Grassington in the west and Ripon to the east; Harrogate is at its south-west corner and Middleham is the northerly point. Within this compact area there are 55 glorious miles of unspoilt paradise. In the first half of his book, John presents a selection of essays that brings to life the landscape, history and characters of Nidderdale. The second half contains 18 circular walks from four to nine miles through the dramatically beautiful landscape of Nidderdale. Concise, detailed route guides include accurate maps, together with at-a-glance details of local amenities and places of interest. Photographs — many in full colour — capture the beauty of Nidderdale and will transport even those who wish to explore the area from the comfort of an armchair. *£7.95*

WALKS IN THE SECRET KINGDOM:
North Northumberland
Edward Baker

With its rugged coastline and miles of lonely moorland, Northumberland is England's borderland, once the edge of the Roman Empire and the focus of centuries of Anglo-Scottish conflict. *£6.95*

NORTHUMBERLAND TOWNS AND VILLAGES
Lydia Speakman

The essential guide to this history-rich county — a comprehensive reference book highlighting the key buildings, landscape and wildlife of the area, together with the stories and legends associated with each community. Perfect for visitors, and those interested in their local history. *£7.95*

All of our books are available through booksellers. In case of difficulty, or for a free catalogue, please contact: SIGMA LEISURE, 1 SOUTH OAK LANE, WILMSLOW, CHESHIRE SK9 6AR.
Phone: 01625-531035
Fax: 01625-536800.
E-mail: info@sigmapress.co.uk
Web site: http//www.sigmapress.co.uk
MASTERCARD and VISA orders welcome.